# The
# Committed
# Life

An Adaption of *The Introduction to the
Devout Life* by St. Francis de Sales

◆ ◆ ◆

William A. Meninger

Continuum
New York  London

2000

The Continuum International Publishing Group Inc
370 Lexington Avenue, New York, NY 10017

The Continuum International Publishing Group Ltd
The Tower Building, 11 York Road, London SE1 7NX

Printed in the United States of America

Library of Congress Cataloging-in-Publication Data

Meninger, William.
    The committed life : an adaptation of The introduction to the
devout life by St. Francis de Sales / William A. Meninger.
        p.   cm.
    ISBN  0-8264-1321-8      0-8264-1285-8 (pbk)
    1. Christian life—Catholic authors. 2. Meditations.   I. Francis,
de Sales, Saint, 1567–1622. Introduction à la vie dévote. II. Title.
    BX2350.2.M44   2000
    248.4'82—dc21                                       00-031403

*This book is gratefully dedicated
to my sister, Patricia Apruzzese*

# Contents

## PART TWO
### *Prayer and the Sacraments*

## PART THREE
*Living Out Your Commitment*

## PART FOUR
### Dealing with Temptations

## PART FIVE
### *How to Renew and Preserve*
### *Your Commitment to Christ*

# The Committed Life

# PART ONE

✦ ✦ ✦

*On Being a Christian*

## ✦ 1
## *True Commitment*

It is a wonderful thing, my friend, to seek to be committed to Christ. It is an unfortunate thing that a distinction is made between being a Christian and being committed to Christ. They should mean the same but they do not. It is socially acceptable today to take on the veneer of Christianity. Without standing in judgment, it is obvious that many people claim to be Christians who do not lead Christian lives. This is evident in the political arena, in the entertainment world, and even, God forgive us, among the clergy, both high and low. It is true also among our own peers.

It is important to understand what commitment means if we are to avoid falling into hypocrisy, a danger to which we are all subject. Commitment to Christ is not defined by subjective whims, false self-systems, or arbitrary morals. Rather, it is holistic, embracing every aspect of life and the pursuit of all the virtues, social and personal.

Too often, it seems, people consider themselves to be Christians when, in fact, they are only following some self-willed, personal obsession. To detest alcohol, for whatever reason, has no Christian meaning if you also detest alcoholics. To give alms, however generously, if you do not also extend forgiveness to your enemies does not manifest Christian commitment. To pray often and at length is meaningless if you harbor ethnic prejudice or hatred. To desire the coming of Christ so that others may be judged and you vindicated does not manifest God's love.

True commitment, my friend, comes from only one source: the love of God. It is indeed that very love that shows itself in all the many facets of our human existence. It is this love that allows itself, through the action of the Holy Spirit, to move us to loving activity consistently, generously, and eagerly. This is the expression of true Christian commitment.

There are three kinds of birds in terms of their ability to fly. Ostriches are strong, ungainly, and speedy. They are also earthbound. They never leave the ground to soar towards the heavens. Like them are people who know only material pursuits. They may expend great energy and cover a great deal of ground but are earthbound. Other birds, like chickens, can fly but with effort, awkwardness, and only at low altitudes. They are people who make periodic attempts at seeking God and serving one another, but without true commitment. Finally there are eagles who soar aloft with swiftness and grace. They arise from the earth yet know how to make the heavens their home. These are truly committed Christians. Such are you called to be.

If we love God, we will keep his commandments. When we allow that love to express itself in commitment, we keep his commandments generously, eagerly, cheerfully, and even with certain ease in the area of crosses and temptations. Commitment does not seek the bottom line, the minimum that we can get away with. It would never model itself after the rich young man whom Jesus loved and called to give up everything for that love but who walked away sad because he was attached to his many possessions. Commitment goes hand in hand with a kind of spiritual aerobics. It is exercised with strength, vigor, and alacrity even in the face of physical weaknesses.

## ✦ 2
## *The Value of Commitment*

In the Book of Numbers, the Hebrew people were called upon by God to make a commitment. This was not to be done blindly. As instructed by the Lord, Moses had sent out twelve men, one from each tribe, to spy out the land of Canaan to see whether the inhabitants were strong or weak, whether the land was rich or poor, the cities were camps or forts, and to bring back some of the produce of the fields, especially grapes, as it was the harvest season. After forty days they returned with their report. It was indeed a rich land, flowing with milk and honey. They brought with them a single cluster of grapes so large that it had to be carried on a pole borne on the shoulders of two men. However, the cities and the men who dwelt in them were also large. Indeed, the men were of such great stature that the spies saw themselves like grasshoppers beside them. It was a discouraging and evil report. It was, they said, a land that devoured its inhabitants.

This, my friend, is the way our world discourages commitment. While it has to admit the values that Christian commitment seeks, it presents them as negatively as possible. Those dedicated to them are often sweepingly presented as hypocrites, dour faced misanthropes, or ignorant fanatics.

Joshua and Caleb, who had been among the spies, were encouraged by God's grace in the power of the Holy Spirit, and protested that it was a goodly land. If the Hebrews committed themselves to overcoming it under the favor of the Lord, it would not consume them, but would be like bread for them to devour.

So the Holy Spirit assures us, especially by the example of holy Christians, that the committed life is a happy one, pleasant and agreeable. The world only sees externals and puts her values on material possessions. Yet in some strange ways the world is forced to honor those committed to serving the poor, bearing wrongs patiently, or striving to restore a sick ecology. Thus she pays tribute to such committed Christians as Mother Teresa or the recent religious martyrs of Algeria. At the same time, in her living example, she encourages us to run in fear from those worthwhile commitments she sees as potentially devouring her selfish pursuits.

Commitment and the virtues required to pursue it do not present to us an unreal world. Hardships, trials, and sufferings are very much present to real Christians. God's gift of love, however, will turn them into joy. It will encourage the poor to work for better lives; it will call the lonely to share in the labor and lives of the community; it will inspire the rich to seek real treasures in heaven by sharing their goods; it will summon the proud to acknowledge God as the beginning and end of all their gifts.

Believe me, my friend, Christian commitment brings love to its true perfection. It is the flower of the plant, the aroma of the ointment, and the brilliant sparkle of the true diamond.

## ✦ 3
## *Commitment Is for Everybody*

Just as the plants of the earth bring forth fruits each according to its kind, so Christians are expected to bear fruit each according to his kind, her call, and their talents. Our abilities differ and our talents vary, as do the circumstances of our lives. Monks are committed in one way, blue-collar workers in another, students and farm workers in still other ways. We can all profit from each other in our multiple ways of commitment but every vocation is special in what it is called to do, how it is expected to serve, and in its contribution toward bringing about the full accomplishment of God's kingdom. Different ministries flow from the very nature of the Body of Christ and are the glory of the Christian people.

True Christian commitment, my friend, honors one's state in life, one's abilities and responds beautifully to God's call. It summons forth unity in diversity, provides complimentarity and fulfills the almost infinite variety of needs in the Church and the world.

Every way of life is called to service and can respond to the demands of true Christian commitment. Christian lifestyles go hand in hand and it is equally helpful, necessary and joyful to grow food (to feed the hungry), to teach (to instruct the ignorant), build houses (to shelter the homeless) or to support all of the ministries through prayer.

The Christ-life, my friend, is open and available to everyone everywhere. What makes a particular lifestyle superior to another is not what one does or even how highly one's calling is esteemed by others. Superiority comes from love and the commitment love summons forth. In this way the last may indeed be first.

## ✦ 4
## *Spiritual Friendship*

> A faithful friend is a sturdy shelter
> he who finds one finds a treasure.
> A faithful friend is beyond price
> no sum can balance his worth.
> A faithful friend is a life-saving remedy,
> such as he who fears God finds (Sir. 6:14 f.).

Spiritual guidance in some form is very important, my friend, if you are to be a faithful, committed Christian. St. Bernard claims that those who provide their own spiritual direction have fools for directors. As important as it is, having a spiritual guide is also problematic. In the traditional sense, a spiritual director was usually a priest who had a reputation for being wise, experienced, and holy. He also had to be someone who had the time and willingness to give himself to the demands of spiritual direction. Such men are rare.

Fortunately, today the notion of the spiritual guide is not so limited. Many nuns now take on this spiritual ministry with generosity and wisdom. Lay people are also receiving qualifications that enable them to take on the roles of pastoral counseling and spiritual direction.

It may be difficult for some people exposed to the more traditional roles of spiritual directors to accept the modern practice of counselors and directors who may even expect financial remuneration for their services. However, this practice is probably not a bad idea. We are accustomed today to pay for such things as physical therapy, body building, diet counseling, massages, and so forth. We appreciate what we receive all the more in proportion to what it costs us. Why not then expend our financial resources for something that is really more important than our physical well being? This is probably a good attitude to cultivate.

However, it is often not possible for everybody who wishes it to have a clerical or professional spiritual advisor. It may be that some form of spiritual friendship will be the answer. This would be a relationship with a friend precisely for the purpose of spiritual sharing. There should be a mutual agreement that certain set times would be exclusively dedicated to spiritual matters—apart from other times and activities given to the friendship itself.

Spiritual direction, for the most part, consists of an attentive, sympathetic, and non-judgmental listening. This is followed by a feedback that basically repeats what the director has heard. Many problems are answered in the accurate formulation of the questions. A primary activity in spiritual direction is simply listening, being a sounding board on whom others can try out ideas, opinions, or self-criticism. The director can then help the directee make objective judgments about his or her own attitudes or possible courses of action. This is almost a natural response to deep friendship. By making such friendship spiritual by a specific agreement of both parties, you will truly find "a treasure beyond price and a life-saving remedy."

♦ 5

## On Spiritual Aerobics

If, my friend, you are committed to physical health and well being, you know well the value of aerobics. You also know that, to be effective, aerobics must be faithfully practiced. At first, the effects are small, becoming more significant as we persevere in them. Then the results are maintained by a regular, faithful regimen. Should they be neglected for a long period, our efforts will have been useless. Commitment is crucial.

So it is with Christian commitment. It is a gradual process brought about step by step with patience and effort. Even when there is a sudden and grace-filled conversion from an unloving way of life to a true commitment to Christ, there comes a testing time when hard work and dogged perseverance will be necessary. It is like the coming of dawn and the dispelling of darkness: it is gradual but noticeable. We must seek a middle ground somewhere between anxious discouragement as we recognize our continual imperfections, and a false sense of achievement in claiming a sanctity that proceeds only from our false-self system. Like a bird who tries too soon to fly we can leave our nested security only to fall.

Spiritual aerobics will be necessary as long as we desire to oppose the debilitating effects of our unloving tendencies. This should not discourage us. In fact, the battle we wage and the victory we seek depend upon our awareness of our weaknesses. We will not consent to these imperfections as long as we continue to oppose them. We will certainly be wounded at times, but never defeated. With God's help the battle will never be too much for us.

As Christians we realize the inevitability of falling. The just man or woman is not one who never falls. Indeed, the psalmist warns us that the just person falls seven times a day. We are just because we get up seven times a day. Spiritual aerobics consist in starting over again as often as is necessary. If we can look back on a lifetime of starting over, we will be successful in our Christian commitment.

## ✦ 6
### *Strength in Our Commitment to Christ*

There are many ways given to us, my friend, to strengthen our commitment to Christ. One way which is helpful at times is to review our past life in order to recall the circumstances which have prompted us to unloving activity. We should look at this unloving activity and try to understand how it affected others close to us. Unlovingness is simply another word for sin, but it somehow embraces the personal element of sin in that it includes the very concrete experience of the wounding or total destruction of relationships. Just as union with God in love and union with all of God's creation in love is a foretaste of heaven, so wounded or destroyed relationships are a touch of hell.

Remember what unloving relationships have done to you in the past. Be aware of how they have harmed others. These memories should not be allowed to depress or discourage you, but rather be the means of a mature self-knowledge calling you to a firmer purpose of amendment. When the circumstances invite you, this could even be a topic to discuss with a soul-friend, a subject to be brought to the sacrament of reconciliation or an issue to be unfolded in journal keeping.

# ✦ 7
## *Attachment to Past Sins*

When the sons and daughters of Israel were delivered from their slavery in Egypt, they at first felt a sense of freedom. They could now be their own persons and pursue their own preferences, profit from their own labors, and direct their own destinies. It was not very long, however, before the burdens of their freedom and the weariness of their journey turned their hearts back to Egypt. Their noble aspirations and lofty self-image began to evaporate in the desert air. Somehow the abject slavery, forced labor, and physical discomforts which impelled them to escape their Egyptian bondage were almost forgotten and they longed "for the leeks and onions" they had in their captivity. It seemed to them that they were better off in their bondage.

Do we not sometimes find ourselves in their position, my friend? A former way of life which God's grace has led us to abandon and which we came to detest once again tries to draw us back into its sinful embrace. Its attractions lure us and the efforts we are making to truly love God, self, and others do not seem to be worthwhile.

If we want to embrace the committed life, we must not only leave behind our unloving ways, but also our attachment to them. Instead of allowing them to make us weak and discouraged, we should use such attachments to impel us forward. They should make us turn to God and place all our hopes in him. It is not a weakness but a strength on such occasions to throw ourselves on God's mercy and to operate out of his strength. Listen to his invitation and his pleas: "Come to me all you who labor and are heavy burdened, and I will give rest to your souls." Leeks and onions, in whatever form they take, cannot do this for us. Repudiate their attractions and open wide your arms and your hearts to a loving God. Then you will know the meaning of St. Paul's paradox, "When I am weak, then I am strong."

## ✦ 8
## Getting Ready

The first step in getting ready for a life of genuine Christian commitment is an honest, realistic look at what our unloving activity has done and can yet do. This will give power to our determinations for the future not only to turn from sin but also to free ourselves from attachments to it. The stronger and more vigorous we are in our attitude toward unlovingness, the more decisive and effective will be our ability to dispel it from our lives. Insofar as it is possible, we must root out sin and the attachment to it from our hearts. The following meditations are suggested as helpful. Do one of them each morning and allow it in some form or other to dwell in your mind and heart throughout the day. You may go longer but ten or fifteen minutes may be enough.

## ✦ 9

## First Meditation: The Totality of Our Dependence on God

1. In your own words acknowledge the presence of God and his grace which now calls you to prayer.

2. God speaks to you. Listen to him.

Then God said, "Let us make man and woman in our image, after our likeness. Let them have dominion over the fish of the sea, the birds of the air, and the cattle, and over all the wild animals and all the creatures that crawl on the ground." God created man in his image; in the divine image he created them; male and female he created them (Gn. 1:26 f.).

3. Read this passage again slowly.

4. Be with this message quietly for a few minutes. Open your heart to receive what God tells you.

5. God is love. This is why he created you. Do you allow yourself to be in his image and likeness? Consider one or two ways in which you have allowed his image in you to be sullied. Speak to God about this.

6. What is your greatest attachment that interferes with your imaging God? Speak to God about this.

7. Carry this phrase (or a similar one) with you throughout this day: "I am made in God's image.

## ✦ 10
### *Second Meditation: Why Am I Here?*

1. In your own words acknowledge the presence of God and his grace which now touches your heart and empowers you to pray.

2. God speaks to you. Listen to him.

> It was not you who chose me, it was I who chose you to go forth and bear fruit. Your fruit must endure, so that all you ask the Father in my name he will give you. The command I give you is this, that you love one another (Jn. 15:16 f.).

3. Read this message from the Lord again slowly.

4. Open your mind and heart to receive these words personally. They are spoken to you.

5. God made you to love and he made everything else in your life to make love possible. Is this the way you see everyone and

everything in your life, past, present, and even future, as making love possible? Can you realize how utterly useless it is to have any other goal? Everything leads to God . . . everything!

6. You are called to love God, yourself and others. When and how have you neglected to do this? Speak to God about this.

7. Carry this brief prayer (or a similar one) with you throughout today.

"My God, everything leads to you."

## ✦ 11
## *Third Meditation: The Gifts of God*

1. Acknowledge the presence of God and, in a few words, ask him to speak to your heart.

2. Listen to God as he speaks:

> Look at the birds in the sky. They do not sow or reap, they gather nothing into barns; yet your heavenly Father feeds them. Are not you more important than they? Learn a lesson from the way the wild flowers grow. They do not work; they do not spin. Yet I assure you, not even Solomon in all his splendor was arrayed like one of these. If God can clothe in such splendor the grass of the field, which blooms today and is thrown on the fire tomorrow, will he not provide much more for you? Your heavenly Father knows all that you need. Seek first his kingship over you, his way of holiness, and all these things will be given you besides (Mt. 6:26 f.).

3. Read this passage a second time slowly.

4. Realize that the Lord is speaking to you. What is he telling you in response to your own particular circumstances?

5. Everything is a gift from God. He brings good out of everything. Thank him for the wonders of your being. Your past with all of its crosses and its joys are all gifts. The greatest gift, however, is the gift of God Himself. What concern should you have then for lesser things?

6. Speak to God about the ways you have put your hopes or desires on something less than him.

7. Carry this prayer (or one of your own making) with you today: "Thank you, Lord, for all your gifts."

# ✦ 12
## *Fourth Meditation: Unlovingness*

1. Praise God for touching your soul and calling you to these moments of prayer.

2. Hear what God says to you in this inspired psalm:

Have mercy on me, O God, in your goodness; in the greatness of your compassion wipe out my offense. Thoroughly wash me from my guilt and of my sin cleanse me. For I acknowledge my offense, and my sin is before me always. Against you only have I sinned and done what is evil in your sight (Ps. 51).

3. Read it again slowly.

4. There is really only one sin as there is really only one commandment. The great commandment is to love God, self, and neighbor. The great sin is to be unloving to God, self, or neighbor.

Examine your conscience in this light. Ask God for forgiveness.

5. The blessed assurance that God does forgive you can be a powerful impetus to thrust yourself into your future with hope and love.

6. Speak to God about your unloving tendencies. Tell him how you want to be compassionate and forgiving even as he is.

7. Carry this or a similar prayer with you all day today: "Have mercy on me, O Lord."

## ✦ 13
### *Fifth Meditation: Death*

1. Place yourself in God's presence and acknowledge his grace, which has called you to this meditation.

2. Listen to the word of God speaking to you:

> My dignity is borne off on the wind
> And my welfare vanishes like a cloud.
> One with great power lays hold of my clothing;
> By the collar of my tunic he seizes me;
> He has cast me into the mire;
> I am leveled with the dust and ashes...
> Indeed I know you will turn me back in death
> To the destined place of everyone alive...
> My soul ebbs away from me.
> Days of affliction have overtaken me.
> My frame takes no rest by night.
> My inward parts seethe and will not be stilled
> I go about in gloom without the sun (Job 30:15f).

ON BEING A CHRISTIAN • 33

3. This is a difficult message to receive. Read it again slowly.

4. Your death is the only absolutely certain reality of your life. How incredibly foolish it is to act as if it were never going to happen. All of the concerns of our lives, all of the material and psychological paraphernalia with which we surround ourselves and clutter up our existence will, in a simple moment, be utterly useless. Do these things help us to serve God? If so, they are useful; if not, they are chasing after wind. Place yourself at the moment of your death and make an inventory of the things that concern you. How worthwhile are they?

5. For your own sake, speak to God about the certainty of your death. Say now the things you would like to be able to say at the moment of death. You have this opportunity now; you may not have it then.

6. Carry this prayer with you today: "All is vanity, except to love God."

## ✦ 14

## *Sixth Meditation: Judgment*

1. Place yourself in the presence of your loving God. Ask him to help you.

2. Listen as he speaks to you:

> Do you not know that God's kindness is an invitation to you to repent? In spite of this, your hard and impenitent heart is storing up retribution for that day of wrath when the just judgment of God will be revealed, when he will repay each of us for what we have done: eternal life to

those who strive for glory, honor and immortality by patiently doing right; wrath and fury to those who selfishly disobey the truth and obey wickedness (Rm. 2:4–7).

3. Read this word again slowly and take it to heart. Sit with it quietly for a few minutes.

4. Speak to God in your own words. How do you wish to respond?

5. God really does not need to judge. When you are in the presence of Infinite Truth, your own truth will be the judge. What you have chosen in this life, you will receive. Look at the things you have preferred before God. Are you willing to have them—and only them—for eternity? Realize that your heart was made for God and it cannot rest in anything less than God. Ask God for the gift of himself right now that you might receive him forever.

6. Carry this prayer (or a similar one) with you throughout this day: "My God, you are the Way, the Truth and the Light."

## ✦ 15

## *Seventh Meditation: Hell*

1. Place yourself in God's presence and ask him for the gift of understanding.

2. Listen as God speaks to you:

> If your hand is your difficulty, cut it off! Better for you to enter life maimed than to keep both hands and enter Gehenna with its unquenchable fire. If your foot is your undoing, cut it off! Better for you to enter life crippled than to be thrown into Gehenna with both feet. If your

eye is your downfall, tear it out! Better for you to enter the kingdom of God with one eye than to be thrown with both eyes into Gehenna "where the worm dies not and the fire is never extinquished" (Mk. 9:43 f.).

3. Read this word again slowly, keeping in mind that in it God is speaking to you. What is he saying? Sit quietly for a few minutes to give yourself the chance to listen.

4. Many of us are in denial when confronted with the teaching on hell. Are we justified in denying the truth contained in it on the basis of the imaginative mythology in which it has been couched? Hell is to choose not-God and to receive it, no matter if it is pride, wealth, power, sex, security, or escape from responsibility: To chose anything less than God will result in hell. God does not condemn us to hell, we choose it! Is it worth it? What does it profit me if I gain the whole world yet suffer the loss of my own soul?

5. Speak to God, admitting the created things that you have preferred before him even if only temporarily. Remember you get what you seek. Seek only God. Tell him right now that he is the only rest for your heart.

6. Carry this prayer (or a similar one) in your mind and heart today: "My God, I choose you!"

## ✦ 16
### Eighth Meditation: Heaven

1. Allow yourself to be in God's presence. Feel him calling you to himself in love and compassion.

2. Listen as God speaks to you:

No eye has seen, no ear has heard, no mind has conceived what God has prepared for those who love him, but God has revealed it to us by his Spirit. The Spirit searches all things, even the deep things of God. For who among us knows the thoughts of anyone except that person's spirit within him? In the same way no one knows the thoughts of God except the Spirit of God. We have not received the spirit of the world but the Spirit who is from God, that we may understand what God has freely given us (1 Cor. 2:9f.).

3. This is probably the most important message God has for you. Listen to it again and give yourself time to let its meaning sink in. So many people today have low self-esteem. They have not been loved at some time in their life as God wanted them to be. They carry throughout their lives feelings of being undeserving and unloved. This is *not* God's message for you. You are loved and God is calling you to a future filled with hope and love. Give yourself to this right now! Thank God for it. Don't let anything less than God into your heart. Truly you and God want the very same thing. Admit it and embrace it. Speak to God openly and honestly, as you may never have done before. Tell him that you want to love him even as he desires and that you want his promise of eternal life in his presence to be your daily hope and consolation.

4. Let this be your prayer today: "My God, my all."

## ✦ 17
### *Ninth Meditation: Choice of Heaven*

1. Place yourself in the presence of God where you know that you can make no other choice but God.

2. Listen to the word of God, as God speaks to you:

> This day I call heaven and earth as witnesses that I have set before you life and death, blessings and curses. Now choose life, so that you and your children may live and that you may love the Lord your God, listen to his voice and hold fast to him. For the Lord is your life (Dt. 30:19f.).

3. Listen once again to these words. Read them slowly and let God reveal the meaning to you.

4. All creation is backing you in your choice for God. Everything in your life is leading to this, even your sins and failures. Everything leads to God. Let it!

5. Tell God—for your own sake, not for God's—how you can see (or how you cannot see) the major events of your life as leading to him. Include here even your sins, failures, and crosses. Ask for the grace to understand how everything! everything! everything! leads to God.

6. Carry this prayer (or a similar one) with you throughout this day: "Lord, you have made me for yourself."

## ✦ 18
### *Tenth Meditation: Making a Commitment to God*

1. Know that you are in God's presence. Express this knowledge to God in your own words and ask for God's help.

2. Listen now to God as he speaks to you:

> Then I saw new heavens and a new earth. The former heavens and the former earth have passed away, and the

sea was no longer. I also saw a new Jerusalem, the holy city, coming down out of heaven from God, beautiful as a bride prepared to meet her husband. I heard a loud voice from the throne cry out: "This is God's dwelling among men. He shall dwell with them and they shall be his people and he shall be their God who is always with them. He shall wipe every tear from their eyes, and there shall be no more death or mourning, crying out or pain, for the former world has passed away" (Rev. 21:1f).

3. Read this again slowly. Let its meaning sink in.

4. Can you make this personal? Can you understand and feel that this message is given to you? You belong in the new Jerusalem. God will wipe away every tear from your eye. Desire to share in this promise so much that you will let go of anything or anyone who would weaken that desire or lead you away from it. Tell God this in your own words.

5. Make now a commitment to put God first in your life. Realize that your heart was made for God and that you will never find rest or satisfaction in anything or anyone except God. It is time to stop dabbling around. It is time to make first things first, to pursue God will all your energy and being. It is time for a conversion, for a total, unconditional commitment. Ask the Blessed Virgin Mary to be your model and your special help. Ask her to show you what commitment means and to lead you along the way it summons you. Do this now. She is waiting!

6. Make this your prayer today and often in the future: "Be it done to me according to your will."

## ✦ 19
### General Confession

At this point, my friend, a general confession is a good idea. Let me, however, extend the meaning of this practice in a way that goes beyond the traditional understanding. By this term we usually mean going before a priest in the sacrament of reconciliation and repeating before him in a general or particular way all the sins of our past life, in spite of the fact that these sins have already been forgiven.

I have some cautions about this practice. You must understand that it is not required of you. At times and for certain people, it is not even helpful. It has been suggested in the past to make such confessions only at certain crucial junctures in your life journey such as marriage, the beginning of a commitment to the religious life or the priesthood, and so forth. You may do this if you feel it to be worthwhile for you in your commitment process.

If you do not wish to make such a confession in the traditional sense, do not be concerned. It is probably not the way for you to go. The idea behind it, however, is a good one and deserves some serious consideration.

We have all heard that "confession is good for the soul." Even specifically non-religious groups such as Twelve Step programs for alcoholics require at a certain stage for the participants to seek out someone with whom they feel comfortable and reveal to this person everything they have done in their life that was negative, reprehensible, or sinful. This is not done for the purpose of receiving absolution (although it can be done for this reason), but for the unburdening of personal secrets weighing down one's heart and soul. It is a way to escape the dangers of our tendency to deny.

You could, my friend, do this if it appeals to you as a general confession before anyone you like. You could also make a personal, private review of your sins. Write them down if you wish and then burn them with a sincere prayer of sorrow before God. Or you could just confess them in prayer before God, leaving them in God's healing hands and loving heart. Again, however, I must insist that you do this, in whatever form you choose, only if it seems to you to be a positive, helpful step in your commitment to God! Otherwise it is best to simply omit it altogether.

## ✦ 20
## *A Resolution toward Christian Commitment*

I acknowledge your presence, O God, and your grace, which calls me to this moment. I gratefully reach out and warmly receive the support and inspiration of the entire Body of Christ. The resolution I now make is not a new one. It was made for me at my baptism and reaffirmed many times throughout my life as I attempted to live out my commitment to Christ.

I admit my failures. Instead of using things and loving people, I have done just the opposite. I have preferred creatures before you as though they were my last end and the goal of my existence. I have violated the great commandment and have been unloving to you, my God, to myself, and to others.

Listen now to my heart's desire. I wish to live in your image and likeness in which I have been created by nature and redeemed by the grace of Jesus Christ. I regret and deplore the unlovingness of my past. I place my weaknesses in your loving hands, accept your generous forgiveness, and resolve to move forward with my hand always in yours.

I have no illusions, Lord, that I will walk in perfection but, at least, I will walk in a faith and a love that will call me to rise instantly whenever I fall. I will not allow discouragement to sully my hope, doubt to weaken my faith or separation from you to destroy my love. I will turn to you in my mornings, my afternoons, and my evenings. I will try to be aware of the abiding presence of your Holy Spirit and when I forget, I will count on you to remind me.

I believe that this resolve that I now make is itself the fruit of your grace. I make it with joy, without holding back, with hope, without discouragement in the union of love to which you call me. I seek the example and intercession of the holy Virgin Mary and of all your saints. I make this resolve in the name of Jesus Christ, my Lord.

## ✦ 21
## *God's Response*

I know it sounds bold of me, my friend, to present to you what I feel God's response is to the commitment you have just made. Yet in his revelation to us in the Scriptures and in the tradition of his church he has made known to us exactly what his response would be. It goes something like this: "My child, I love you with an everlasting love. I love you with the love of a mother, a father, a brother, a sister, a child, a husband, a wife, and a friend. Indeed any time you experience love from any of these relationships, know that it is just a pale reflection of the love I have for you. Who better than I is aware of your weaknesses, your sins, your inadequacies, and your failures? Yet when I look upon you, I do not see this shadow side. Rather I see from and with the light who is my beloved Son, Jesus Christ. I do not see your sins or the scars of your wounds. I see only the light and life and the victory that Christ has won for you. Reach out and embrace this victory, claim it for yourself and boldly accept the personal and intimate union I offer you. In fact, you have done this in the resolution you have just made for a Christian Commitment. Place your hand in mine and we will go forward in confidence, grace, love, and power. Please realize from the bottom of your heart that I do not judge you as the world judges. All that I judge is your desire to come to me. Are you poor, are you alone, are you ill, are you ashamed, are you powerful as the world sees powerful? Are you rich, young, healthy, surrounded by friends? None of this matters. You are my beloved in whom my favor rests. Arise, my beloved, and come."

Please, my friend, it is so important that you take this to heart. No matter what your past or even your present, your future reaches out and summons you with the power of God's Holy Spirit. You are loved and loving, happy and free in God's life-bestowing grace. No matter what your earthly circumstances are, you have everything that really matters. You have God! Let me help you further in the subsequent chapters of this book to live out your union with God. May God bring to a perfect fulfillment what he has begun in you this day.

## ✦ 22
## On Being Free to Love God

What is it then, my friend, that we look at? Where do we focus our attention? We are called to mirror-image the likeness of God. Yet God's light which accompanies this mirror-image is so perfect and pure that it reveals the tiniest imperfections. At the same time that it reveals our inadequacies, it calls us to desire more and more to be purified and perfected. What is our concern then? Is it attachment to sin, from which we will never be entirely free in this life, or is it attachment to God?

Look to God, my friend, with the light that comes from God. You will see what there is in yourself that is God-like and you will see, at the same time, what is not-God, your attraction to sin. Both are real but they are not of equal power. Allow your love for God to overwhelm you. Let it spread throughout your being, your emotions, your thoughts, your body, and your soul. Consciously live in this love. Turn your face to God. Be generous in God's love and in your own.

# ✦ 23
## *Freedom from Stupidities*

Stupidities, my friend, are useless and dangerous pursuits that not only are a waste of time but which can lead to love-destroying activity. Our society is oriented to such vanities. There are movies that are questionable in the explicitness of their sexual portrayals, TV programs in which violence is rampant, and computer games and web-sites that cater to our baser desires. Books, magazines and public advertisements bombard us with deceiving enticements, presenting them as normal, desirable, and even necessary for social prestige. Amassing material possessions, indulging in the vagaries of fashions, seeking happiness in superficial inanities are daily placed before us as instant imperatives.

Some of these things are clearly wrong for us. Others, perhaps more dangerously, are not obviously immoral but serve to weaken our efforts to live lovingly, filling our minds and hearts with stupidities. Have a care with the time and energy you may spend on such ridiculous and profitless pursuits

# ✦ 24
## *The Struggle against the False-self System*

All of us, my friend, have personalities that God once saw coming from his creation as being very good. However, as we enter into the human environment our goodness is distorted or bent. We call this original Sin. It means that we have, in addition to our gifted-ness, a shadow side that obscures our real self and distorts our noble call to God's image through the power of the Holy Spirit and the grace of Christ.

Our false self-system often takes those very gifts that God has given us and uses them to distort his Image. This is done by stress-ing them too much or by not acknowledging them at all. Virtue stands in the middle and too much or too little of a good thing destroys it. In the next section of this book, I will present you with the multiple aids that God gives us to help us in our struggle.

# PART TWO

✦   ✦   ✦

## *Prayer and Sacraments*

# ◆ 1
## *Our Need for Prayer*

My friend, we must be aware first of all, that we are the one's who need prayer. God does not need it. He has gotten along without our prayer since the beginning of time. He wants us to pray, however, because we of our very nature need it.

I am, of course, speaking of prayer in a much wider sense than the commonly held idea that it consists in asking God for favors. Two of the more important things that prayer does for us is to open our minds and open our hearts. Ignorance that belongs to the mind and base desires that belong to the heart or will are dispelled by prayer. Through prayer we come to a true knowledge of God, and open our minds to know him and ourselves further. Through prayer we also are led to desire and choose truth, goodness, and loving activity over the selfishness our false self would have us choose.

Scriptural meditation is especially important for us, using the Lord as our inspiration, teacher, and model. "Learn of me," Jesus tells us, "for I am meek and humble of heart." He is also the Truth and the Way and the Light of the world. He offers himself to us to enlighten our choices and to recognize the truth about ourselves, our worlds, and our Father.

Without Jesus, my friend, we walk in darkness. With him we are led to the Father in the graciousness of his Holy Spirit. As the Divine Word made human, Jesus speaks of the Father to us in ways we can understand and imitate. We are called to become one with him even as he is one with the Father.

It is therefore especially recommended that we use the gospels as an aid to our mental prayer. This, of course, includes the commentaries and reflections of such spiritual writers as Thomas Merton, Thomas Keating, Henry Nowen, Megan McKenna, and others, as well as the traditional classics of Christian spirituality.

It is well to form a human habit of spending some time each day on scriptural meditation. We have daily habits of carrying out our basic human needs such as washing, eating, and sleeping: Should we not also include as a part of our routine such an important practice as prayer? A special time and a special place for our mental prayer can be important. Even as brief a time as ten minutes with the Scriptures each day is worthwhile. Make this your minimum, always allowing for the possibility of going for a longer period. Chose a place where you are not likely to be interrupted and where you can settle down comfortably. Always be open to different possibilities for a suitable place when you are not at home, such as. a church, a park, a waiting area in an airport, a bus station, or elsewhere.

Simply speaking to God in your own words or through traditional vocal prayers such as the Our Father or the rosary is also important. This kind of prayer will have a different place in your life as your needs change but should not be overdone or neglected entirely. Some people may feel that they have gone beyond the need for this kind of vocal prayer but this is really unlikely. Others may think that vocal prayer is all there is and that the more time they spend in reading prayers or repeating memorized prayers, the holier they are. Should such prayer become tedious or difficult over a long period of time, we must recognize the need to change our dominant form of prayer. It is also to be recognized that one Our Father said slowly and devoutly is better than many said in haste. Vocal prayer is often useful as an introduction to other kinds of prayer, such as scriptural meditation or the prayer of the heart (which we shall deal with later). Sometimes when we find it impossible to spend time in mental prayer we may want to give a bit of emphasis to a simple vocal prayer we carry with us through our busy day. We should not, however, give in to discouragement if we have neglected our scriptural meditation. We can always begin over again today (never tomorrow).

## ✦ 2
### *The Presence of God*

There are many ways, all of them valid, my friend, to practice mental prayer or, as I prefer to call it, scriptural meditation. By personal practice you will find what is the best way for yourself. It is also useful to know several different ways so you can vary your practice when it suits you. Whatever method you use, the first step is always placing yourself in the presence of God. I would like to suggest four possible ways of doing this.

The first way is found in the answer to that very basic question often seen in children's catechisms. "Where is God?" The reply, of course, is "God is everywhere!" Like many simple statements, this one is also very profound. God is infinite and limitless and therefore must be everywhere. In regard to yourself, then, my friend, it is important to realize that God is especially everywhere that you are. Listen to how beautifully this reality is expressed in Psalm 139.

Where can I go from your spirit? From your presence where can I flee?

If I go up to the heavens, you are there; if I sink to the nether world, you are present there.

> If I take the wings of the dawn, if I settle at the farthest
> limits of the sea,
> Even there your hand shall guide me, and your right
> hand hold me fast.
> If I say, "Surely the darkness shall hide me,
> and night shall be my light."
> For you darkness itself is not dark, and night shines as the
> day.

We know this, of course, but because familiarity breeds contempt, we are all too often not aware of it. We must remind ourselves frequently of God's presence, especially as we begin to pray. It is also a great consolation to remember that when we make the effort to recall God's presence we are doing so in response to God's grace. "No one can say, 'Jesus is Lord,' unless he be given the power by the Holy Spirit." This is in itself a testimony, God-given, to his presence. When you begin your meditation say with great conviction, "My God, you are here."

The second way to be aware of God's presence is to realize that he is closer to you than you are to yourself. He resides at the very still point of your being. That you exist at all means that you share in his being. St. Paul reminds us that "In him we live and move and have our being." The psalmist expresses it beautifully.

> O Lord, you have probed me and you know me;
> You know when I sit and when I stand;
> you understand my thoughts from afar.
> My journeys and my rest you scrutinize,
> with all my ways you are familiar.
> Even before a word is on my tongue,
> behold, O Lord, you know the whole of it.

Behind me and before, you hem me in and rest your
hand upon me.
Such knowledge is too wonderful for me;
Too lofty for me to attain (Ps. 139:1–6).

Recall also the beautiful prayer of St. Patrick in which he
acknowledges the all-pervasive presence of God. "Oh God," he
prays, "be before and behind me. Be above me and below, on right
side and left. Be within me and without." Is not this kind of presence to be expected of lovers? Union and presence is the language
that belongs to you and God.

The third way to realize God's presence is through the risen
humanity of Jesus sitting at the right hand of the Father. He sees and
knows all that the Father sees and knows. He and the Father,
through the communicating action of their Holy Spirit, touch all
reality, especially us, the children of God, redeemed and given new
life in Christ Jesus. Indeed we are incorporated into the very Body
of Christ. Wherever we are, there is Christ!

Yet a fourth way to make us aware of the presence of God is to
remember Jesus' promise that he is with us all times, even to the end
of the world. There are many manifestations of his Real Presence: in
the sacraments, especially the Eucharist, in the read scriptures, in the
gatherings of the faithful, and in the individual soul, to mention but
a few.

So you see, my friend, there are many ways in which you can
present yourself to the presence of God as you begin your prayer.
Indeed, this practice, if it appeals to you, can be your very prayer
itself. Just be still and in an awareness of God's presence. At times
nothing more is necessary.

## ✦ 3
## *Ask God for Help*

When monks and others chant the praises of God seven times a day in the divine office, they always begin by asking God for help. "Oh God," they sing, "come to my assistance. Oh Lord, make haste to help me." This is what we should do in our meditations once we realize that we are in the presence of God. Sometimes we can be overwhelmed by that presence. Sometimes we can be in such spiritual aridity that it means very little to us. In either case the best response is to turn to God for help. This is very simple to do. Just like the monks, all we need do is to ask Him in our own words. "Please God, help me to spend these few minutes in your presence responding to your graces." Try to realize as you do this that God is already answering your prayer. It is not out of place here, if you so desire to place yourself in the loving hands of the Virgin Mary, or your patron saint.

## ✦ 4
## *The Next Step: Use of the Imagination*

Many of the Church Fathers and Mothers, anticipating the marvelous instructions of St. Ignatius, the Founder of the Jesuits, suggest that we bring all of our faculties into our meditations. These include our emotions, imagination, intellect, and will. Try this and see if it helps you (sometimes it may not be useful, especially when you are in the process of entering contemplative prayer). Suppose you are meditating on a passage from the gospels. Place yourself in the setting of the passage (Nazareth, Bethlehem, the Sea of Galilee). Feel the place, hear the voices, smell the scents, imagine the surroundings, the view, the people, immerse yourself with the sound of the Lord's words. Be there! There will be times when you are called to go beyond all of these considerations. Don't be concerned when that happens. Simply let it be.

## ✦ 5
## *The Meditation*

I am sure you realize, my friend, that at this point you are already immersed in your prayer. You can see that what you are doing is significantly different from mere reading or even deep study. You are opening your mind and heart to God and the things of God. You have already done this in the ten meditations I have outlined for you. Remain peacefully open with your considerations of any teaching, mystery, or incident in Jesus' life that you are dealing with. Stay with it as long as it speaks to you. Do not hesitate to move on when nothing more is being offered.

## ✦ 6
## *Decisions Resulting from Meditation*

The real purpose of meditative prayer, my friend, is to move you to action. You make use of your faculties, memory, imagination, emotions, and intellect in order to move your will to make decisions according to God's grace. Your meditations will move you in wonderful ways toward love of God, self, and neighbor. You will experience compassion for the suffering of others. You will feel a growing desire for God's kingdom even now in your daily life. You will be led to true sorrow for past unlovingness.

All of this is very good. But you must keep in mind Jesus' admonition: "Not everyone who says to me, 'Lord, Lord,' will enter the kingdom of heaven, but they who do the will of my Father will enter the kingdom." Your decisions must be concrete and practical, directed towards very specific persons and events in your life that call forth your compassion, forgiveness, or any of the corporal and spiritual works of mercy that the situation warrants. Are you moved by your meditation to a spirit of amendment because of your unlovingness? To whom have you been unloving? How? What will you do today to repair it?

## ✦ 7
### How to Conclude Your Meditation

You may wish to end each meditation by expressing simply, in your own words, your gratefulness to God for the grace by which he called you to your prayer. State before him, again in your own words, precisely what you have gained by your meditation. Even if you seemed to gain nothing, tell him so! Finally, tell him what you intend to do, this very day, as a result of your prayer. To remind yourself of your meditation and concrete resolution, it is a good idea to take either some small part of your meditation, a word or a phrase from the Scripture you used, or a very simple prayer in your own words that can easily be repeated through the day. You can look at the ten meditations given earlier in this book for examples of resolutions.

# ✦ 8
## *Some Helpful Advice*

To speculate on virtues that we do not put into practice in our daily lives leads to deception and pride. So it is important, my friend, to make the fruits of our meditation practical. This means that we have to seek out in a positive and active manner opportunities to apply our resolutions.

Seeking these opportunities will also be a significant aid in another problem that faces us when our period of prayer is finished. Sometimes it seems that we have to move from one dimension of reality to another when our prayer is over. From a situation of relative or profound peace, with our concerns focused on God and God's will in our lives, we must move back into the confusions, noises, and cares of our every day preoccupations. Not only the duties of our state in life but the problems of our jobs, our environment, and our personal well-being quickly take over to fill our minds and hearts with busy-ness. Herein lies the value of actively seeking in the midst of these occupations real situations where we can apply the fruit of our meditation. Also we can see here the value of the above mentioned simple prayer that can carry us through the day with a grace-filled connection to our time of meditation

# ✦ 9
## *Spiritual Dryness*

There are times, as you have already experienced, my friend, when your prayer will be difficult, full of distractions, restless, and entirely without comfort. There are any number of things you can do, but our first resolve must be to persevere. Spiritual dryness is God's way of calling you more intimately to himself. It is your chance to prove to God and to yourself that you are seeking God rather than the gifts of God. Love begins when nothing is expected in return. Throw your inabilities before the Lord and tell him of your frustrations. Insist that he help you.

I recall being in such a situation while trying to pray in church. I literally had to hold on to the bench in front of me to remain for the meager ten minutes I had promised the Lord and myself. Other times I would make the Stations of the Cross just going from one to the other with a mechanical determination to say the Lord's Prayer and a Hail Mary at each station. Still other times I would say the rosary, needing to feel the beads going through my fingers to have some assurance that I was praying. Read prayers from a prayer book or the Psalter can be helpful at such times, as well as some fitting physical activity such as kneeling and standing frequently, or even (when alone) making complete prostrations. Often times there is a legitimate and fulfilling satisfaction after such prayer simply from knowing that you have persevered in it.

It would not be unusual if such prayer ends up in a kind of companionable silence in God's presence. This is something that sort of creeps up on you unnoticed even while you are in the midst of your seemingly futile struggle with dryness. Generally you will not be aware that this has happened until it is over. It is the beginning of contemplative prayer and often is the fruit of perseverance in prayer amid the distress of spiritual dryness.

## + 10
## *Daily Prayer in the Morning*

Prayers do not have to be lengthy. Jesus reminds us, "In your prayer do not rattle on like the pagans. They think they will win a hearing by the sheer multiplication of words" (Mt. 6,7). Remembering that we pray for our own sake (not for God's), ask yourself what brief sentiments are useful for you to place before God on a daily basis soon after waking up. Because they will be brief, these prayers can be said as soon as you wake up. You can even say them while you are in the shower, dressing, or shaving. Of course, if it is your custom and you find it helpful, you may pause in your activities and say them while seated or kneeling. Consider the following ideas for prayer as possibly helpful, or use your own. Probably one or two of them briefly stated before God is enough.

1. The morning offering is a wonderful way to begin the day. Offer the whole day to God; all its blessings and crosses, successes and failures. This was once a very popular devotion. It is worthy of preserving. Use any memorized form or use your own words. Make it brief: "Lord, I offer you this day, myself, and all that I do."

2. Thank God for creating you, for giving you this day and for loving you. This can be simply expressed and repeated throughout the day: "Thank you, Lord for everything."

3. As I have already mentioned, it can be very helpful to run your mind ahead to the people, situations and events you will deal with today. In this way you will be better prepared to act with God's love and to use his grace in each situation. As simple as it is, this practice can be of enormous help.

4. Call upon Our Lady to help you. A simple "Hail Mary" or even a part of it will suffice. Commend yourself to your patron saint or to a heavenly favorite: for example, "St. Francis, pray for us."

5. Use your imagination to vary this routine. Pray for different people who have special needs in your world as they occur to you. Remember, do not overdo it. Keep it fervent and brief.

## ✦ 11
## *Evening Prayer*

Evening prayer can be similar to morning prayer. However, if you have other practices such as meditation, scripture readings, forms of lectio divina (spiritual reading and reflection), this can be an adequate substitute for evening prayer. How often people berate themselves for having forgotten or skipped evening prayer. There is no need for this. You can simply commend yourself to God as you go off to sleep. There is no real need to kneel down or to "cover" certain intentions. If you have a routine for evening prayer that works, continue it. If you are, like many people, unorganized, simply say a brief prayer—even as simple as, "Thank you, God, for today." If you have trouble falling asleep, this is a good time to have a prolonged conversation with the Lord.

## ✦ 12
## *Daily Recollection*

My friend, some kind of practice of daily recollection is of great importance. How quickly time can go by without our giving even a brief thought to the most important reality of our existence, the presence of God within us, around us, and in the person of everyone we deal with. It's obvious that frequent awareness of God in our daily lives has an important influence on our motivations and our actions.

No one ever has to know about this. It can be done literally in an atom of time. Yet it can transform you and your day. A fleeting thought expressed in your heart in a few simple words done frequently through the day can have a value far surpassing the effort it takes. A practice like this, my friend, will not permit you to hold on to anger, to plot revenge, or to give in to despair. It will bring you moments of hope in difficult situations, a ray of sunlight in darkened corners of your day, and allow the power of the Holy Spirit to break into your life.

Hold on to some prayer-phrase or verse from Holy Scripture such as was suggested in the meditations given earlier in this book. Call on the Lord. Reach out frequently to grasp his out-stretched hand whenever anger, impatience, unkindness, personal inadequacy, misunderstandings, or overwhelming duties confront you. God is with you. He is an ever-present help in time of distress.

# ✦ 13
## *Simple Ways to Be Recollected*

Be aware of God, my friend. Realize that God empowered himself to enter dramatically and concretely into our human situation by taking flesh in our Lord, Jesus. He understands our frustrations, our sufferings, our consolations, and our joys. Refer them all to him. Do it often.

Referring oneself to God frequently during the day in simple heart-felt phrases such as: "My Jesus, Mercy," or "Lord, be with me," or even a brief prayer for others such as "Lord, comfort him," or "Lord, be with her," are wonderful ways toward recollection. Let your emotions direct your brief prayers. Follow your heart whenever you experience love, sympathy, pity, or hope. Know that these sentiments are the product of grace and let them call forth from you frequent simple prayers.

One very wonderful way to be recollected and mindful of the presence of God is by what has come to be called the Jesus Prayer. It goes like this: "Lord Jesus Christ, Son of God, have mercy on me, a sinner." This is said together with your breathing until it becomes virtually a part of it. Whenever you are doing indifferent things that do not require concentration, such as walking, jogging, or waiting for a bus, let this prayer come forth. At first this will have to be done deliberately and consciously. After a while it will be as natural and as frequent as your breathing. I know a man who has been saying the Jesus Prayer for thirty-three years. Whenever his mind is free of serious occupations, the prayer comes about by its own power. Even when he is concentrating on something, it softly and gently repeats itself in the background, surfacing whenever a lull in occupation occurs. When he awakes in the morning it is the first thing to come to his consciousness. When he waits for sleep in the evening it is the last thing on his mind. A good way to learn more about this prayer and how to make it a part of your life will be found in the lovely book *The Way of the Pilgrim,* written anonymously by a monk of Mt. Athos in Greece.

St. Therese wrote somewhere that she did not believe that more than three minutes of her day went by that she did not acknowledge the presence of God. It is the custom among Muslims never to speak of any event to be done in the future without adding on the phrase "If God is willing." The ways to be reminded of and to acknowledge God's presence in your world are countless. Everything around you speaks of God, even the sinful and ugly, as it calls forth pity, understanding, and love. Remember also that even if you forget God, God will not forget you.

◆ 14
## Weekday Eucharist

The practice of assisting at daily Mass has, for centuries, been one of the most important and sanctifying customs in the church and fortunately it remains so today. Done together with others in religious communities or in parish families, it is the fullest liturgical expression of what it means to be the Body of Christ. Perhaps you cannot do it on a daily basis but it may very well be possible on occasion. Use weekday liturgy as a special celebration of events or people, living or dead, in your life. Attend Mass and receive communion on birthdays, family, and civic celebrations, in response to personal and worldwide needs, or on an occasion when you know a legitimate reason may prevent you from a Sunday liturgy.

Consciously join in with the prayers of the priest and the congregation. Make every effort to make the worship sincere, enthusiastic, and effective. A careful attention to the liturgy will give you an awareness of the meaning of the liturgical seasons, the feasts of the saints and, above all, the life-bestowing love of Jesus Christ who died, rose again, and who will come in glory. Through him, with him, and in him offer to the Father, in union with the Holy Spirit, the fullness of his own honor and glory.

✦ 15

## Devotions: Public and Private

As you are well aware, my friend, there are available to you endless devotions both public and private. Follow your attractions reasonably and sincerely. The rosary, Stations of the Cross, various novenas and the like can be very helpful in your spiritual growth and expression as they appeal to you. Be aware, however, that the church offers these devotions on a personal level. You may share your joy and appreciation of a particular devotion with others, but always do it in a reasonable and deferential way.

Some people, in a misguided enthusiasm, present certain private devotions to others as though they were indispensable for salvation. They even use false promises or supposedly divine threats uttered against those who do not succumb to their personal attractions. Sometimes their methods, while sincere, are improper theological interpretations. Just as one unfortunate example, one often sees printed prayers to the Blessed Virgin or to St. Jude accompanied with the statement: "This prayer has never been known to fail." The truth of the matter is that any prayer, properly understood and properly offered, has never been known to fail. However, the impression conveyed is often that of some magical, superstitious value attached to a select group of words which will then get for you anything you want.

Unfortunately there is today an unhealthy flutter of activity revolving around questionable apparitions of Christ, the Blessed Virgin, or the angels. These must be approached with circumspection and a reliance on the decisions and advice of church authorities. Be mindful that extraordinary manifestations of the supernatural call for a certain common sense and dignity. Be wary of good intentioned but gullible desires to experience the extraordinary. I do not think it is a good theological stance to see the work of the Holy Mother of God in altering film negatives or video tapes to show questionable "apparitions" not otherwise seen. Look primarily to Christ, to the scriptures, and to well authenticated apparitions for your devotional resources.

# ✦ 16
## The Communion of Saints

One of the most beautiful and consoling teachings of the church, my friend, is that of the communion of saints. Through the redeeming power of Jesus Christ and by the graciousness of the Holy Spirit, we are personally bonded with one another and with each grace-filled soul created by God. Through distance, through time, and through dimensions of reality, the oneness, the love, and the personal relationships are present by the power of the Holy Spirit who is, as it were, the very soul of the Mystical Body.

We have the memory, the experience, the intercession and the example of all the members of Christ's body both living and dead. Cherish this union and allow the intimacy of these holy persons to be a part of your life. From the holy Mother of God to the most recently baptized infant, we have an intimate and personal family relationship. Our patron saints do take an interest in us. We always have something for which to rejoice in the graces, gifts, and successful work of others.

# ✦ 17
## *The Holy Scripture*

God is present where his word is read and heard. This is especially true during the Eucharistic Liturgy. When the gospel is finished, the priest says: "This is the word of the Lord." We respond: "Praise to you, Lord Jesus Christ." We acknowledge the Real True Presence of Jesus Christ in reading and listening to his word.

Let your faith remind you of this great gift even when you take up the Scriptures for your personal reading and meditation. Speak to the Lord in your own words and listen to him in his own words. Such a great privilege! Present an open mind and heart also to the writings of others who tell of their own experiences and reflections on the Sacred Scriptures. Share also your own encounters with God through his holy word. This can be done by belonging to a scripture discussion group or by your personal sharing with a soul friend.

## ✦ 18
## *Personal Graces*

Everybody knows the story of the man who was promised a visit by the Lord. He prepared himself and his household for the Lord's coming. Every other duty and occupation was temporarily put aside so that all would be ready whenever the Lord appeared. As he waited, an old beggar knocked at his back door to ask for food. "I'm sorry," the man said, "I usually do respond to the needs of the poor, but today I am awaiting a special visitor and must be ready to receive him whenever he arrives." Then his phone rang and it was a friend asking for a favor to help him in an immediate need. Again the man put him off with his excuse of a special visitor. As the day went on there were three more requests for help or for time-consuming favors, he refused them all for the same reason.

As the day came to a close, the Lord still had not arrived. Finally, disappointed beyond measure, the man gave up hope and prepared for bed. Before falling asleep he appealed to the Lord in prayer and asked him why he did not come to his home as he promised. From somewhere within the depths of his heart, he received an answer.

"But I did come," said the Lord. "In fact I came four times and even telephoned you once. Each time, however, you refused me."

We must be aware, my friend, that it is in such unassuming ways that the Lord makes his presence known to us. We receive many, many graces in the course of our day, that bring the Lord into our lives. Every holy inspiration, every inclination to practice a corporal or spiritual work of mercy, every sympathetic movement toward the trials of others, every moment of sadness for our sins and those of our world is an announcement of the Lord's coming to us. At this point we are free to receive him, or, as the man in the story did, to reject him.

In point of fact, every single thing that happens to us is a grace, a notice of an impending visit from the Lord, if we receive it correctly. What a joy this can be! To know and to respond to everything . . . everything . . . as leading us to God!

Life for a Christian, my friend, can be a perfect joy. This is true even though it will often involve trials, pains, and suffering. Through hope, joy is present in our crosses when we have the faith to see them as a share in the cross of Christ. Even our sins can lead us to God. As St. Augustine said, "I could not love you so much, Lord, had I not sinned against you so grievously."

So, my friend, expect the Lord to visit you. Take pleasure in his graces and inspirations and recognize him in his gifts and in the least of his brothers and sisters. Share this awareness in a practical way, with an advisor or a soul-friend to assure yourself of the authenticity of God's presence in the practical graces of your daily life.

## ✦ 19
## *The Sacrament of Reconciliation*

The theology of the Sacrament of Reconciliation and the concrete practice of the same sacrament in its liturgical expressions can be problematic. The theology tells us that the specific sacramental grace of Reconciliation helps us deal with the particular sins and faults we confess. Thus we receive significant help from God in regard to our personal offenses. By way of omission this fact is often presented as though there was no other way these sins can be dealt with. Yet the truth of the matter is that the church has always taught that these sins are forgiven by prayer, almsgiving, and the reception of Holy Communion.

The practice of the Sacrament of Reconciliation has varied enormously over the centuries. Many of the great saints from the first eight centuries of Christianity never received this sacrament in their entire lifetime. Except for rare cases at the moment of death, the sacrament was administered only by the Bishop on Holy Saturday in the public liturgy for the forgiveness of certain scandalous and public sins which amounted to a flagrant denial of one's commitment to Christ—such sins as idolatry or murder. Enormous penances were given. So severe were they that many people put off receiving the sacrament until their deathbeds. Because of the seriousness of their unforgiven sins, this also meant that they could not receive Holy Communion. When private confessions were introduced (by Irish monks) with relatively milder penances, church authorities condemned them. In fact, it was only by force of repeated disobedience to authority that the Sacrament of Reconciliation became a common practice.

Current practice is in a state of flux and there are varying opinions. Some want to continue the practice of the past century or two of requiring the reception of the sacrament either before each reception of communion or very frequently, even weekly. Others wish to take a position between the stricter practice of the earlier centuries and this more recent practice.

Theologically, it has always been maintained that confession was only necessary when a mortal sin has been committed. The problem has been and remains: what is a mortal sin? Serious matter, sufficient reflection, and full consent have been offered as criteria for determining if a sin is mortal. However, with the advent of new knowledge about human nature coming from the behavioral sciences, this can be variously interpreted. Certainly we are more cautious in our dogmatic statements that such and such a thing is a mortal sin. One obvious example of this is a statement from Pope John Paul II in his recent instruction on chastity. He states that masturbation, while always a serious issue, is not to be considered a mortal sin when it is habitually practiced—the reason being that habit diminishes sufficient reflection and full consent.

This is not a new teaching but the application of the teaching is new. Fifty years ago, it was simply taught that masturbation was a mortal sin. The role of habit in diminishing reflection and consent was simply ignored. Thirty years ago many priests and nuns who suggested that it might not be a mortal sin (and thus not demanding the Sacrament of Reconciliation) were severely condemned by many. Today the Pope supports their stance!

What are we to say then, and what is our practice to be regarding this sacrament in our pursuit of the committed life? There is obviously room for varying opinions and practices. It is a matter for individuals to decide in accordance with their own inclinations and needs. It must be said that many priests recoil in horror at the thought of restoring weekly confessions with the inevitable, meaningless "laundry list" of sins. It must also be said that there are times when confession is truly necessary. Mortal sins are committed. Forgiveness is available.

For those committed to the Christian life, it is to be expected that mortal sins are rarely if ever committed. This being the case, confession is rarely if ever required. It does, however, play an important place to play if you desire, my friend, true and authentic spiritual growth. There will be times in your life when you will experience a true and deep sense of guilt at some action, relationship, or attitude. It may not fall under the definition of mortal sin but will be important enough for you to feel that it would best be handled through the Sacrament of Reconciliation. Because of the powerful emotional responses to such situations, it will not be difficult to realize when recourse to the sacrament is advisable.

What of other times and situations? Perhaps light can be shed here in terms of an examination of conscience. This should be done on a regular basis whether in preparation for confession or not. If you find the traditional way of examining your conscience helpful— review of the virtues, duties in life, the commandments— then do it.

There is another approach you may also find helpful. Jesus has given us the one, great commandment: to love God, with the totality of your being, body, mind, heart, and soul, and to love your neighbor as yourself. There are then three loves: God, self, neighbor. There are also three sins: to be unloving to God, self or neighbor. You might try using this as an examination of conscience. In what ways have I been unloving to God? Unloving to myself? Unloving to my neighbor?

# ✦ 20
## *Holy Communion*

We have also seen a change of emphasis, my friend, regarding Holy Communion. In fact, we no longer even speak of Holy Communion as some kind of independent, isolated devotional exercise. We speak rather of the Eucharistic Liturgy of which the reception of Holy Communion is an integral part. There is no question that even prior to the Second Vatican Council the church was aware that the direction of Eucharistic understanding and practice had to be modified.

Essential to our understanding of the Incarnation, my friend, is that it is God's way of making himself approachable. The God of the Old Testament was a God whose ways were not our ways. Isaiah said that as far as the heavens were from the earth, so far were his ways from our ways. His name was unspeakable and his presence in the Holy of Holies was unapproachable. Where he did make personal contact with his prophets and anointed ones, there grew up a fear that death would be the inevitable result. To see God was to bring death.

The Word was made flesh and dwelt among us precisely to change all of this. God became one of us that he might make himself approachable! When Jesus died on the cross, the veil of the tabernacle was split from top to bottom and the secret place of the Holy of Holies where God had dwelt in the tradition of his people in awesome and isolated mystery was laid open. God was now to be manifested in the risen Christ and even further in the new temple (not made of stones) of the Body of Christ, the faithful.

Jesus promised that we would be one with the Father and Himself. To bring this about sacramentally he instituted the Eucharist. Through the simple and approachable celebration of His Supper, we could recognize and be one with him in the breaking of bread and the drinking of wine.

Gradually, however, as the centuries went on, the faithful began to ignore the approachability of God and to stress, once again, his awesome transcendence. This became liturgically manifested in the aura of mystery and unapproachability that gradually took over the form of Eucharistic celebration, especially in the reluctance of the faithful to approach such an awesome God in the reception of Holy Communion. It became the common tradition to attend Mass without receiving the Body and Blood of Christ.

This became such a common abuse that the church found it necessary, some five hundred years ago, to enact a law requiring the faithful to receive Communion at least once a year (during the Easter season). Because of the rarity of this annual reception, there was a common feeling (but never a legal or moral requirement) among the faithful that this must be preceded by the sacrament of Reconciliation, even when mortal sin was absent.

It was not until the beginning of the twentieth century that reception of Communion, theologically and liturgically an essential part of the Eucharistic celebration, began to be frequently practiced. It still remained difficult for the church to persuade her members of the approachability of God in the Eucharist. The transcendent element was overstressed by the mysterious language of the liturgy, the very strict demands of fasting from midnight to receive Communion, the unapproachable nature of the celebration with its beautiful but forbidden exclusivity of sanctuary space, its select ministers, the exclusion of women, and especially the stressing of the divine presence in the Eucharist and the consequent unworthiness of anyone seeking to approach Christ in Holy Communion.

I recall vividly, my friend, attending in my younger days the 11:30 A.M. Mass on Sundays in our large parish church together with 1500 others. At Communion time only four or five people approached the altar rail to receive Christ. Even in my early days as a young monk, we celebrated daily a magnificent Solemn High Mass at which we were forbidden to receive Holy Communion! The devotional literature in which we were steeped stressed our unworthiness to receive the Body of Christ. Denying all but the priest the "privilege" of receiving the cup further enhanced exclusivity and unapproachableness. No matter what we did, we were told by the literature that our preparation was inadequate and unworthy. There was no way in which we could approach the altar hearing those beautiful words of Jesus, "Come to me all you who labor and are heavy burdened and I will give you rest," or "I will no longer call you servants but friends." This was true as well after the faithful were encouraged to receive Communion frequently, even daily. What had happened to the approachability of God and the simplicity of the Lord's Supper?

Is it any wonder then that the church especially during and after the Second Vatican Council sought to stress the "horizontal" (approachable) nature of the liturgy and to lessen the transcendent element? Many of us, my friend, deeply loved the older liturgical customs and miss them. This is only natural given the importance of having a liturgy we were accustomed to, and our appreciation of a ceremony of unsurpassed beauty developed over many centuries—although it must honestly be admitted that it was often, especially on a parish level, celebrated without any vestige of that beauty. The transcendental element was also important to us and it was (and for some, still is) difficult for the church to teach and convince us of the need for liturgical reform for the reasons stated above.

To be a truly committed Christian, my friend, we must listen to the church. We must open our minds and hearts to receive the fullness of her liturgical teachings and not make vain, personal, and often resentful efforts to "turn back the calendar." We should also be understanding of the reluctance of those who cannot or will not accept changes at such a deep level of their spiritual attractions. At the same time, if we are to grow in our Christian commitment, we must be open and receptive to the church's guidance in this respect. Our energies should be directed in a positive and loving way as we run forward into the arms of a loving, approachable God who calls us to himself.

# PART THREE

✦  ✦  ✦

## *Living Out Your Commitment*

## ✦ 1

## *The Variety of Virtues and the Call to Commitment*

There is, my friend, an interesting study of human personalities called the Enneagram. The word means "nine points" and describes the theory that there are nine responses possible (but in almost infinite combinations) to the fundamental human need for love. We are born with a need for love and respond to our environment, apparently urged on by certain elements in our DNA, in basically one of nine different ways to get this love and its accompanying security and approval.

According to traditional Christian spirituality, the desire to give and receive love, basic to every human being, manifests itself because of Original sin through the Capital Sins. Together with deceit and fear, the seven Capital Sins help form the basis for the nine types of human personality. Because of the "bentness," or, as theologians call it, "the wounds in our natural faculties," we over-stress one particular way of achieving our needs. Thus, each us is prone to a "favorite sin," a vice intended to secure a good thing—love—but one that has gone astray. Accordingly, traditional Christian spirituality assures us, we are called to the virtue opposite our particular vice or Capital Sin.

All of the Capital Sins present a danger as well as a challenge to all of us, but, in accordance with our personality, there is one that each of us must be especially aware of. In general this is easy to understand. If you are tempted to pride, my friend, it is obvious that humility is the virtue you must strive for and are called to, especially by your Christian commitment.

We will take a brief look at each of the nine personality types as understood by the Enneagram profile. Be aware that you have a share in each type (and perhaps will recognize yourself in them), but there is one type in particular that may suggest itself to you as dominant and thus involved in the sin most particular to you. Thus you will know what virtue you are specially called to practice in order to counteract that sin. Remember that the Capital Sins plus fear and deceit are not actually sins in themselves but are tendencies toward sin.

One type of personality is the perfectionist. The perfectionist feels and thinks that he can only receive love if he correctly fulfills the expectations of significant others in his past or present life. He is under a compulsion to do everything correctly, as he perceives perfection to be. His sin is anger and resentment at a world that does not live up to his expectations. It is a hidden sin because he seldom will allow himself to express or even admit the imperfection of his anger. He is called to the active and deliberate pursuit of discernment to realize that the world and himself must be loved and appreciated for what they are rather than for what his unreasonable expectations demand. He is especially called to peace and serenity in the face of an imperfect life and environment.

Another type of personality is that of the helper or the server. This person neither realizes nor accepts herself as loveable. To be loved she is under a compulsion to do things for others, even to the detriment of her own needs. Her sin is pride. She takes pride in what she wants to perceive as her selflessness. She is imprisoned by the needs of other people and will resort to flattery, especially when she feels unable to help them in genuine ways. She is called to a freedom where she will accept herself as lovable not for what she does for others but for who she is. She must work for the freedom to see the truth about herself and to accept that truth. This is the virtue of humility.

Yet another type of personality may be called the achiever. He thinks that others will love him only if he is successful. He therefore must be at the top of the heap in whatever he does. His major goal in life is to best others to the point that he will never even admit to failure. His sin is deceit and a vanity that seeks to hide weakness or inability. He must actively pursue the virtue of honesty which will allow him to face the truth about himself and to accept the hope that he is worth more than merely what he does.

Another kind of person is the one addicted to specialness. This person must be unique and different from others in everything she is and does. Only by giving into the addiction to uniqueness does she feel that she will be loved. Her sin is to envy everyone and everything she thinks to be more special than she is. She surrenders to melancholy as she regrets her present experience and longs for the idealized past or the unattainable future. She must work to achieve the balance or equanimity to be authentically original, without prejudice to others.

There is a reflective or thinking type of person who seems to dwell exclusively in his mind. He thinks that he can survive and call for the love he needs by having all the answers, usually on a theoretical level. His time and efforts must be spent on acquiring knowledge rather than on sharing it. Thus his sin is stinginess and avarice. He must struggle to overcome this compulsive greed and is called to practice generosity in sharing his knowledge. He has to do this by involvement and participation in his world in the face of his inclination to detached withdrawal for the sake of observation.

Another type of person lives in a world of fear. He seeks love in security and the structures that an organized group offers him. Fear is the basis of all his decisions and can manifest itself by flight or aggression (usually unreasonable). He tends to be cautious over consulting or adheres too strictly to rules. He needs to work hard to obtain the virtue of courage and the faith in himself that it brings. He must see the value to be found in structural and social support but nonetheless he also must learn to stand on his own two feet with confidence.

It may sound like a good thing to be an optimist but this next type of personality, like the others, sins by excess. For him life can be secure, approving, and loving only when he succeeds in avoiding pain in all its forms. He strives compulsively to see only the bright side of things and plans assiduously for a life of pleasurable gluttony, and thus refuses to realize the place and value of crosses and the need for hard effort. Temperance and industry are the virtues he must use to counteract his ephemeral dallying and search for the pleasurable.

There is also a type of personality that can be called the boss. This person, like the others, prompted by certain recently identifiable elements in his DNA and in response to environmental considerations, is convinced that he will be loved only by demanding it, by taking care of his own life (and often the lives of others). His compulsion is to be confrontational and demanding. He must be in charge. His sin is the excessive demand for power, which we call the Capital Sin of lust, together with a proclivity toward vengeance when this is frustrated. He is called to work for the expression of truth and the moderating influence of innocence.

The final personality type we will consider can be called the laid back mediator. This laid-back type discovered that the best way for her to get security and love was to avoid conflict at all costs. She feels than an indifferent attitude toward life and a hands-off approach is best. Her sin, which supports this mind-set, is sloth. Obviously she is called to overcome this addiction by active hard work and the motivation of a supportive, interested love for others.

As I have already indicated, my friend, we all share in all of the tendencies represented by these personalities and their accompanying Capital Sin. However, you may be able to identify one of them as describing the area of your own particular personality. This will be a great aid to you in knowing precisely where you must apply yourself and on what virtues you must work.

# ✦ 2
## *Further Advice on the Virtues*

Beginners, my friend, must start at the beginning. We must be moderate with them and with ourselves. As we advance in our Christian commitment, we will become more and more sensitive to our faults. We will also become more and more sensitive to how far we fall short of the perfection of God, whose image and likeness we are being brought by grace to restore. There is even a paradoxical sense in which true growth in Christian commitment simply brings us to an awareness of the imperfect success and fumbling nature of our attempts at living the virtues. Thus we constantly feel that we are only beginning, even while we are running along the path towards God.

Thus we should not be discouraged, but willing to start again each day, even seven times each day. I do not know of any single principle that can be as helpful as this if we only take it to heart. We must seek moderation with ourselves and with others. Virtue stands in the middle and our tendency is to sin either by excess (a form of lust) or by defect (a form of sloth).

At one time spiritual writers used to delight in placing before their readers stories of the extraordinary graces given to the saints. It seemed that those ecstasies, visions, and levitations were being placed before us to imitate or, at least, as indications of how far we fall short of real holiness. An emphasis on such things, my friend, is dangerous.

Our lives are filled with extraordinary graces and wonders. Simply look about you and observe the heroic efforts of simple Christians to patiently accept their illnesses, tragedies, sufferings, and crosses. Look at the daily examples of heroic sanctity shown in the love of unpretentious and unassuming people for one another. They are all around you, my friend. Be one of them. Blessed are you when you have not seen (the extraordinary) and yet believe. God will do great things with you, through you and by you if you seek to remain meek and lowly of heart.

## ✦ 3

### *Patient Endurance*

My friend, this is not a popular subject. Probably because of that, it is all the more necessary that we confront it directly and honestly. I am not sure that I am comfortable with the Catholic tradition that gives such a prominent place to the crucified Jesus—I mean this in contrast to the Protestant custom of displaying a simple plain cross. Both practices are justified, of course, and it is simply a matter of emphasis.

When we take up our own crosses daily and follow Jesus, is it to his death or to his resurrection? Obviously it is to his resurrection *through* his death. We have no problems with accepting the resurrection. No doubt this is why our tradition emphasizes the crucifixion. Both are profound expressions of God's love who died for our sins and rose for our justification. At this moment we shall deal with the cross as it represents the very real sufferings of our life, never forgetting, however, that its purpose is to lead to resurrection.

It may be that at times the pious and even deeply spiritual literature of the church is too much for average sinners such as you and me. We read of the saints embracing their sufferings with joy and eagerness because their faith assures them of the salvific power of their pains when joined to the sufferings of Christ.

Joy and eagerness are not words that most of us can associate with our crosses. Probably patient endurance is as close as we can get. There are times when we border on or even give in to despair. We call on God in our pain and there is no answer. We seek light at the end of our tunnels and there is only darkness. Even though it offers little consolation, our faith tells us that at no time in our life are we more closely connected to Jesus when he cried out "My God, why have you forsaken me?" If we were, at this moment, visited with consolations, our crosses would not be real. We can only cry out with Job, "Even though he slay me, yet I will trust in him." There will be times when we have gone through the dark tunnel and emerged into the light that we are given to realize that God was with us in the darkness, but we could not experience him. There will also be a time when the cross will lead to our physical death and our emergence into the light that will be our resurrection.

There is a very real sense in which we can say that it is not God's will that we suffer. He is like loving parents who, so that their children grow into maturity and independence, will not remove every difficulty from their path, but are watching over them the whole time, whether the children realize it or not.

Does the virtue of patient endurance allow us to complain? I think that it does. How else can we interpret Jesus' cry on the cross? Complaining to God is even a form of prayer as long as it is accompanied by the bottom line Jesus gave us. "Father if it is possible, let this chalice pass from me, but not my will but yours be done."

As love dictates, we should do everything in our power to alleviate our pains. It would be a sin of presumption to do nothing and expect God to intervene. He will help those who help themselves. The classic motto applies here: We must work as though everything depended upon ourselves and pray as though everything depended on God. The bottom line is to see God's will in the results of our work and prayer no matter what those results are.

We can also complain, vent our feelings, or release our tensions to a reliable and trusted friend or spiritual companion who realizes what we are doing and who will support us in a difficult time. This is true also of certain organized groups whose very function is to provide a safe environment for our grievances.

Remember that there are always those who are worse off than you. Your sufferings, whether physical, mental, economic, or spiritual can be of service to the world as you unite them to the Body of Christ and make up what is wanting in his sufferings. He has won the victory for us but it is painful, at times, to reach out to claim it.

# ✦ 4

## *Humility about Possessions*

Now, my friend, we will look at another unpopular topic: humility. If we are to allow God's grace to restore God's image and likeness, much of which we have lost, we must look at the truth, which alone will set us free. That is what humility is—an acknowledgement of the truth, the truth about ourselves and all that we have and are.

The opposite of humility is pride (sometimes called vainglory). This is the vice we give into when we arrogate to ourselves something that belongs only to God. We use the word pride in several senses, one of which need not be sinful. Thus we speak of being proud of our country's efforts to help the poor, or being proud of our public parks or our children's efforts at school. When we give thanks to God for such things, we know that our pride is not sinful, that it is not vainglory.

Sinful pride or vainglory can be so subtle or habitual that we are not even aware of it. We can have an abiding attitude of pride because of personal or family wealth, because of an elaborate wardrobe, because of expensive cars, position in society, various artistic talents, or even physical attractiveness. Accidental frivolities such as a pleasing countenance, an attractive mustache or hairdo, the ability to dance well, a good singing voice, skill in athletic games, are stupid vanities when seen as something that calls for personal adulation. To modestly cultivate such things and use them in God's service without undue attachment would be a truthful and humble response to them.

Even richer gifts can lead to pride if not seen as coming from God and useful for God's service. Learning, whether scientific, secular, or religious; the adulation of followers and popularity through the mass media, if seen as due to yourself as a result of your own efforts, can all be sources of pride. Ecclesiastical honors, the pomp and circumstances of hierarchical ceremony, even liturgical ones, pose a danger of believing they are given to honor oneself rather than God. Such things rightly viewed will lead to humility. Honor given to us because of a gift or talent rightly used is to be accepted gratefully. When it is sought after, demanded or expected as due to one's own creative capacity rather than God's gifts, it is a superficial preening of peacock feathers! Who can, by his own power, add even a fraction of an inch to his own height?

# ✦ 5
## *Real Humility*

As real humility is a simple acknowledgement of the truth about ourselves, it also calls for a certain acceptance of the gifts God has given us. We must honestly face our virtues as well as our vices. To deny our God-given talents and even the labor we have expended to develop them is to minimize God's love for us. Such an acknowledgement can be humbling.

Only God is good so every good thing can come only from God. All the good things we have, we have received. Why should we then take inordinate pride in them? To acknowledge God's gifts will not only make us humble, it will make us grateful. How beautiful Mary showed this attitude. She admitted, in her humility, that she glorified God who had done great things for her. She sang of God's gifts and of the gracious role God had given her to show forth the splendors of God's glory. Indeed, paradoxically, it was because God recognized her humility that she could be glorified.

Because humility is truth, we must avoid any semblance of phoniness. There are certain types of people for whom this is a particular danger. People who are success-oriented must beware deceit. They find failure, great or small, very difficult to face so they hide it under the guise of a pretended success. For such people, failure is sometimes a special gift of God because it is the only way they can be made to admit their dependence on God and be led to humility.

False humility is a danger to be aware of. I have seen it often, my friend, in people who refuse to receive Holy Communion because, as they say, they are not worthy. It is precisely the reception of communion which makes us worthy, because of the union with the Body of Christ, to which God graciously calls us. Any who feel that they are worthy of themselves (because of the way they live) are by that very fact unworthy!

There are some holy people who are known for having hidden their God-given virtues because of a great desire to abase themselves in the practice of humility. I do not judge such people but I would rather admire than imitate them.

# ✦ 6
## *Humiliations*

Someone has said, my friend, that the only way to humility is through humiliations. We will have them. There is no way they can be avoided. However, rare is the man or woman who can actually desire them for the sake of the virtue they can produce. Perhaps the best we can say is that humiliations are inevitable and we might as well make the best of them by accepting them and allowing them to lead us to true humility.

In our society today, the simple attempts to live openly and honestly as a Christian is a humiliation. We are called often to take unpopular stands on public issues such as abortion, the death penalty, military interventions, government attitudes in foreign affairs, wasteful neglect of resources, public pornography, and immodest speech and clothing. We do not have to look for humiliations. They will be present in whatever abundance is necessary to combat our personal vainglory. We should take advantage of them, being very careful to examine the truths about ourselves that they manifest. The hardest ones are sometimes the most brutally honest. These are also the most profitable.

# ✦ 7
## *Your Reputation*

My friend, humility permits and charity requires that we be concerned about our good name. Indeed this is, in many ways, the foundation of civil society. A good reputation, honestly deserved and enthusiastically pursued, sets a good example for others and is diametrically opposed to the sin of scandal.

Indeed scandal is so rampant in our day, among the clergy as well as the laity, that it is hardly seen as a matter of concern, yet it is one of those sins that Jesus most vigorously opposed. Better, he said, to be drowned with a millstone tied around your neck than to give scandal. The opposite of scandal is good example. For this a good reputation is necessary. Thus it is virtuous to strive for it.

For this very reason we must also defend our good name when it is challenged unjustly. This will happen. Jesus was so challenged. We must do whatever is required to clear our reputation. On the other hand, we must strive for a certain indifference even in this regard if we are not able to refute unjust charges. Such situations force us to put our trust in God, and, though they are painful, they can be the means of real Christian growth since they call for restraint and even forgiveness. We have had a remarkable example of this in our own day in the response of Cardinal Bernadin of Chicago to public charges of sexual immorality. His attitude of acceptance and forgiveness turned a scurrilous accusation into an occasion for the highest Christian virtue.

It is helpful to remember that our good name results from our love for God. It is the fruit of our desire to please God. While we must strive to defend ourselves against false accusations, we should, at the same time, be consoled by the knowledge that God searches our hearts and knows the real truth. There are times when this may be our only consolation.

✦ 8
*Gentleness*

President Bush called on Americans to become a gentler, kinder nation. This was a very appealing plea. Opposed to this, both in society and in individuals, is the very strong tendency to anger. Anger is what prompts such evils as capital punishment, prison for vengeful incarceration rather than rehabilitation, refusal to compromise politically, and the destruction of loving bonds.

Individual anger often motivates our decisions, even while it is being denied. Some people wear their anger on their sleeves: they are aggressive and confrontational, but others harbor a deep-seated anger that motivates much of their behavior, though they pretend it does not exist. For such people anger is expressed indirectly through non-verbal communications or through passive aggression. These people reveal their anger by intolerance or arrogance when contradicted or accused of being less than perfect.

Over-defensiveness, hurt pride, and forceful retaliation call for true humility and gentleness. How unhappy are those people whose lives, directly or indirectly, are ruled by their anger. How unhappy they make others, especially those closest to them. Even when anger seems justified, it is most often effectively expressed peacefully and gently. More flies are caught by honey than by vinegar. Just as anger, in its unchristian embrace and calls for unpleasant responses tends to capture others, so does gentleness share itself in a powerful, effective, non-threatening way.

The apostle James tells us to "be quick to hear, slow to speak, slow to wrath, for the wrath of a man does not accomplish the righteousness of God." Again we are told in Proverbs, "A mild answer calms wrath but a harsh word stirs up anger." Angry people live in angry worlds because they create them by their anger. Proverbs also tells us, "A fool gives vent to his anger, but a wise man keeps himself under control." We are also told, "For as churning the milk produces butter, and as twisting the nose produces blood, so stirring up anger produces strife."

Anger contradicts reason and belittles it. It befits animals better than it does people, as it seeks to force compliance through fear rather than love. While there is such a thing as reasonable anger or anger motivated by love, we must be cautious in admitting it. It has a way of getting out of control and finding contrived excuses to feed itself, and becomes very hard to drive away.

When anger first shows itself internally, with gentleness and calmness approach it to discourage it. Seek God's help in a brief prayer. This could be a grace-filled way of counting to ten before expressing anger. Try then to respond to the person or situation with deliberate gentleness and see the difference this will have both on you and on others. Do this even (especially) if you have already fallen into anger. It is a good remedy. Have a gentle attitude. When you know you are going to enter a situation that ordinarily would evoke anger, such as a difficult meeting or an unpleasant confrontation, built up a reserve of gentleness beforehand. Let this be what emerges instead of anger.

+ 9
## Patience with Ourselves

Sometimes we are angry because we are forced to live in an imperfect world. Our critical minds see everything and everyone, including ourselves, as flawed and imperfect. Such an attitude is exhausting and we are defeated even before we begin. This is true even when we limit our efforts to correcting the imperfections in ourselves alone—never mind the rest of the world.

The only solution for this is patience. This involves recognition that nothing is really black or white but everything (including ourselves) is a shade of gray. This must be accepted internally. This is how things are, how I am, and it is all right. This does not mean that we condone immorality or cease to correct it but it does mean that we patiently look at the real world and our real selves honestly and compassionately. We are imperfect and we will fail. At the same time we will patiently begin over again after each fall. It is this that will make us successful Christians. Perfection will not do it, because we will never be perfect.

We will know when we are simply trying to rationalize our sins in order to hold on to them. After a fall we must patiently pick ourselves up again, acknowledge our weakness before God in true humility and seek his help once more. God will be satisfied with this. So should we!

# ✦ 10
## *On Overdoing It*

Somebody once said, "Worry is a form of atheism." Rather than being worried about our responsibilities, perhaps we should use the word *concerned.* How blessed we are, my friend, when we can carry out our duties with the confidence that we are working with God. We must be concerned that we do the best we can and confident that God will also. In this way nothing we do will ever be a failure. At times we may seem to be failures—just as Jesus did!

There is a Greek word, *synergy*, which means "to work together with." Let us manage our affairs synergistically, together with God. Then we need never be over anxious about the outcome. My friend, we all find ourselves at times in the position of Martha who was anxious over many things. The Lord has given us a beautiful prayer for such times in Psalm 127:

> Unless the Lord builds the house, they labor in vain who built it.
> Unless the Lord guard the city, in vain does the guard keep vigil.

It is vain for you to rise early, or put off your rest.
You that eat hard-earned bread, for he gives to his
beloved in sleep.

Do what duty calls you to do peacefully and orderly and rely on
God's help. Let go and let God! When an elephant and a puppy are
yoked together to pull a heavy load, is there any need for the puppy
to be over anxious about his share of the burden? Enough said!

# ✦ 11
## *On Obedience*

You may be surprised, my friend, what a large role obedience plays
in our lives. I am not speaking of the vow of obedience made by religious orders, but simply of the normal, everyday type of obedience
that is called for by normal, everyday living. The need for obedience
is stitched, as it were, in the very fabric of our existence. For the
good of society, the welfare of the state, the functioning of the
church, and our own spiritual and physical well being, we must be
obedient. Often this obedience is impersonal like in obeying traffic
laws. Sometimes it is owed as a response to personal needs like when
we take medicine required for physical illness. Again, at times, it is
called for by our particular livelihood, the demands of our work, or
the smooth functioning of our family life. This kind of obedience is
called for impersonally and almost automatically.

Still further obedience is owed to persons who hold positions of
responsibility for the effective functioning of all of these situations.
I am not referring now to any kind of blind obedience such as was
once put forward as a virtue or as is sometimes expected of children.
Obedience should be intelligent, responsible, and willing.

Obedience for the sake of the well-being of our society and personal lives is obedience to God, who graces us with this virtue to facilitate the practice of charity through the tranquillity of order.

We should, my friend, cultivate an attitude of obedience as our normal response to daily existence. This is not always easy. When it is easy, obedience can be the result of laziness or indifference or even servile fear, but it is good to be in the habit of virtuous obedience because love demands it.

At the same time, obedience can paradoxically require disobedience. What this means, of course, is that obedience to a higher authority (and personal conscience, well informed, is our highest authority) takes precedence over a lesser one. This can justify, for example, actions of civil disobedience when unjust laws are in force. Unfortunately, this can be the situation in ecclesiastical as well as state governments. Prudence and prayer are obviously very important in these situations. Having the virtue of obedience as a habitual attitude is a safeguard against specious appeals to higher obedience.

A suspicious, mistrustful, disobedient attitude is often the result of pride. People with this attitude are often unpleasant and difficult to work with. Control freaks are not easily given even to legitimate obedience. Look to your motivations. Are you concerned with the effective functioning of the Body of Christ in the marketplace as well as the church? Our obedience is ultimately a response to the will of God as we reorganize it through grace, discernment, and love.

# ✦ 12
## *On Chastity*

Perhaps nothing has changed so radically in our times as the attitude toward sex and, as a corollary, the attitude toward chastity.

Recently there was an article in a national magazine about a young Christian couple engaged to be married who had promised one another, and their mutual families, that they were going to practice chastity in their courtship even to the extent of avoiding physical touch altogether. This was regarded as so unusual that it deserved national attention.

Sexual rigidity especially in the non-Latin Christian countries certainly went to extremes. This was the logical result of social, cultural and ecclesiastical misunderstandings. Finding a basis in specific Old Testament attitudes and supported by a Platonistic suspicion of the body as distinct from and inferior to the soul, sexual mores were taken to their rigid extreme in Victorian society. The reaction to this came especially in the 1960s and 1970s in the flower child culture with its suspicion, disregard, and hostility to the principles held by parental, civic, and church authorities, even if these authorities themselves ignored their own moral codes. The results that we are experiencing in the twenty-first century resemble a throwing out the baby with the bath water: If attitudes toward sex were unhealthy, extreme, and even inhuman, then there should be no restrictions at all. Chastity became in practice a non-existent virtue. Rationalizations have become rampant to the point that anything goes whether in and out of marriage, and often even in the religious and clerical state.

Somewhere a voice is needed to call us, not back to the inhuman attitudes of past centuries (especially the nineteenth and twentieth centuries), but ahead toward a healthy, holistic, and mature appreciation of both sex and chastity. A significant step in this direction is the motu proprio of Pope John Paul II on chastity.

When we deviate from a proper understanding of God's commands, we deviate from a proper understanding of human nature, human needs, and human maturity. Chastity, properly understood in and out of marriage, is a necessary and indispensable virtue both for individuals and society.

Questions are raised today on sexual issues such as birth control, divorce, homosexuality, masturbation and various forms of sexual practices herefore considered deviant. Not all are easily answered. The voice of the teaching authority of the church must be carefully heard. It is indeed rash and potentially destructive to act contrary to it without mature consideration and prayerful, loving reflection directed toward rooting out the ever-present danger of rationalization and human weakness. Love and do what you will, but be sure the love is genuine. Let every decision proceed from being in God's presence in prayer.

## ✦ 13
### Personal Chastity

St. Paul warns us, my friend, that "among you there must not be even a hint of sexual immorality, or of any kind of impurity." This is a clear situation where the old adage "avoid beginnings" comes into play. Temptations to sins of the flesh, as you know, are insidious, ever ready to blossom forth and subject to all kinds of rationalizations. Our society, our mass media, and our entertainment world constantly thrust them into our faces. It is impossible to avoid them entirely. Nonetheless it is far easier to avoid the temptations than to cure the habit. The habit of sexual license is so strong and immediate that it can be formed by only one fall.

Anything that weakens your resolve to live chastely should be avoided. Sexual activity in the proper circumstances, within the marriage bond, is good and holy in spite of misunderstandings to the contrary. As St. Paul reminds Timothy, "Everything created by God is good, and nothing is to be rejected when received with thanksgiving." Here St. Paul is specifically refuting early heretics who forbade marriages!

Let your attitude toward chastity be a positive one. Let your thoughts, your desires and your senses be set on things above, not on earthly things. It is God's will that you should be holy, avoid sexual immorality, and learn to control your body in a way that is holy and honorable (see 1 Th. 4). Put these things before yourself always: whatever is true, honorable, just, pure, lovely, gracious; whatever is excellent and worthy of praise. Think about these things and the God of peace will be with you (see Phil. 4).

# ✦ 14
## *Spiritual Poverty*

Being rich or poor in today's world, my friend, is a very relative thing. Even many of those whom we would place very low on the scale of material possessions are rich in comparison with the very rich several centuries ago. Things that could be seen as constituting riches are at the disposal of everyone , including public transportation, libraries, social security, Medicare, and public schools. I, myself, was born into poverty but did not even know it until I was almost an adult. I do not deny that dire poverty exists, but even then it is relative. Compare the poverty of the South Bronx with the poverty of Haiti. Riches too are comparative and relative. No doubt there are people (and nations) that are unquestionably rich according to any material standards and yet these same people can be and often are among the poorest of the poor in terms of happiness, peace and a fulfilled life.

I have a friend who visited Mother Teresa in India and offered to remain with her there to serve the "poorest of the poor." She sent him back to the United States where she said he would find even poorer people, such as some who have abortions so they will be able to afford a new car or a vacation.

All of this is why the beatitude speaks of the poor *in spirit*. We will always have inequality of material possessions. This has been so even in so-called communist countries where everything is owned is common.

The poor in spirit are promised as a reward the kingdom of heaven. This is where true riches are found. The difference between the poor in spirit and its opposite, the rich in spirit, lies in attitudes and goals. One can be very poor in material things and yet be possessive, greedy, and unsharing. This is to be rich in spirit. One can have much in material goods but possess them unpossessively as a steward of the Lord's bounty. This is to be poor in spirit.

What is it that you desire? Where are your efforts directed? How possessive are you? How generous are you? What is your reaction when you suffer a loss of material goods? How attached are you to things? Take pleasure indeed in all the things of God's creation but in such a way that the loss of them would not substantially affect your happiness. This is to be poor in spirit and the reward is great: the kingdom of heaven. Do you want anything less?

# ✦ 15
## *We Can Be Poor While Rich*

Poverty in spirit is not a matter of what we possess but how we possess it. A gardener who works on a rich estate but who is truly concerned for his work will be more dedicated to the garden than its owner. This is how we are to possess riches. We should make good use of God's creation and seek to please him as we do so. We act for love of God rather than love of self or love of things.

When our use of things is motivated by self-love or greed we can recognize it by the kind of concern we show. Is it anxious, uneasy, suspicious, and disquieting? If so, our motives are unworthy. On the other hand, does our concern manifest itself peacefully, gently, and even with what can be called holy indifference? If so, we are poor in spirit.

The poor in spirit who have great or relatively great wealth are generous in its disposal. People who tithe ten percent of their income freely and generously are usually happy people lacking greed and acquisitiveness.

It is necessary for all of us to serve the poor, to be somehow among them in our service and to be aware of their hardships. I know a very wealthy man who worked one day a week in a soup kitchen. It was very easy for him to sign a check, he would say, but to be in contact with the poor was another thing.

I know another man who earns an average salary in New York City who never leaves for work without a pocketful of change so that he may never refuse any of the proliferous beggers whom he met on the way. His concern was not on what some would do with his charity but the good it would do others and himself.

The rich should welcome occasions when their wealth does not alleviate their troubles, like when they are ill or traveling in areas not responsive to wealth. It is good to observe your reactions, my friend, when you are inconvenienced by poor service, inadequate accommodations, or inattention. To be grateful when you do not have to put up with such things and to be undisturbed when you do: that is to be poor in spirit.

# ✦ 16
## We Can Be Rich While Poor

If we are materially poor, my friend, we should also be poor in spirit. We can make our poverty a blessing even while we seek reasonably to improve it. To be poor is to be in good company. Be aware of the companionship that is yours, from Jesus to Charles de Foucauld and Mother Teresa; from the early Christians who possessed all in common to St. Francis and present day Catholic worker communities. Make a virtue of it; see its value for your own spiritual maturity.

Do not complain because you are poor, my friend. We only complain when something displeases us. Do not allow poverty to have this effect on you. Let it lead you to work hard, to be grateful for the little you have and to sympathize with those who have less. Do not be ashamed of your poverty, too proud to seek help when it is needed, or too upset when it is refused. For now, at least, it is God's will for you and a clear path toward your salvation.

♦ 17
## *Friendship and Its Counterfeits*

In our relationships with others, my friend, many times we think of "friendship" and "love" as different from each other, but they are really just labels for the same thing. There should be no difference between real love and real friendship. We are concerned here with phony relationships formed from motives that are base and selfish. There can be no real love or friendship unless our motivation is, instead, selfless.

We often hear warnings such as "Friends don't let friends drive while drinking." This is based on the assumption that a real friend will not give into base motives such as peer pressure, indifference, or the desire to keep the peace, and in the bargain allow someone to come to harm, or harm others.

Only recently we experienced a diabolic massacre of fifteen high school students by two of their number who were pledged "in friendship" to destroy as many students as possible. What was the real bond uniting these two depraved killers? It could not have been either love or friendship. We could express it this way. "True friends do not cooperate in activity that is harmful to themselves or others."

To be genuine, friendship must be mutual, and must proceed from a desire to give to the other only those things that would help the other to become the best human being possible. Anything else is counterfeit and a chasing after wind.

◆ 18

*Dalliances*

A question must be raised here, dear friend, about relationships presumably based on love and friendship that take on some or all the privileges and obligations of marriage. This is a modern custom much to be deplored. It has been brought on by the frequency (and acceptability) of divorce in modern society. Couples will "try out" a marriage relationship without the benefits, graces, obligations, or true meaning of the sacrament of matrimony. It amounts to living a lie and little good can be expected of it.

The couples themselves distrust their own love, respect, and commitment to one another. They do not recognize their union as a selfless, loving bond made before God and honored by society. Often such unions are based on merely physical attractions or even only financial convenience. How different they are from the true sacrament that pledges love, honor, and obedience before God and one another, and places a firm and holy trust on each others' word and commitment.

Also to be deplored is the present practice of physically expressing, in unlimited sexual intercourse, a type of union that is simply a sham, and an expression of irresponsible and unbridled lust. Young couples today often, as a matter of course, engage in sexual activity that has true meaning and value only under the marriage bond. Casual dating, even with a stranger, is often expected to include sexual expressions. This is neither love, friendship, nor respect. It is a cooperative endeavor to mutual destruction based on a fleeting sexual pleasure that is selfish and meaningless. Such dalliances exclude true love, respect for God, and honor to humanity.

# ✦ 19
## *Real Friendship*

In one of King David's most beautiful songs, he sings, "Behold how good it is, and how pleasant, where brethren dwell as one!" He sings of real friendship, shared love that desires only what is truly best for the beloved. This kind of friendship comes from God and will last forever in God.

We are subject, no doubt, to many friendship bonds in many different forms. Our relationships with our extended families, our co-workers, our church community, and our neighbors all call for friendliness, but these relationships are shadows of a true loving friendships, bonded by the Holy Spirit and reflecting the very love of God. Such friendships will be rare. We can expect only a very few in our entire lifetime, but they are to be cherished all the more for this reason. In a monastery, religious community, or family, friendship is a reflection of God's love and calls forth the desire to see and support in one another that unselfish, unconditional charity that is God's own gift.

Discernment is needed to recognize and reach out to one another in such friendships. They are called to be good, holy, and sacred.

There is no room for exclusivity or mutual disregard of others. A friendship can be special and particular while still open to others.

## ✦ 20
## *Friendship with the Opposite Sex*

My friend, prudence and caution must be maintained, lest we be deceived about our friendships. This is particularly true with someone of the opposite sex. History abounds with examples of true and wonderful friendships between men and women. Unfortunately, there are even more examples of friendships that began with a virtuous love, but ended in a relationship less admirable.

This is true especially in our times when most people consider themselves mature and reasonable, and capable of nurturing and enjoying a relationship with the opposite sex that will remain platonic. Such a situation is possible, but is often not realized. This is an area in which self-deception and rationalization are easily given in to. If a friendship is to be true, it may only proceed with grace-given prudence and caution. Real friendship lends itself to honesty, kindness, respect, and honor. It should be a reflection of the union of the very saints in heaven.

## ✦ 21
## *Dealing with False Friendships*

In dealing with false friendships, he first thing to do is to avoid their beginnings. Relationships that involve flirtation or lustful feelings should be cut off before they start. This is sometimes hard, because one is apt to rationalize: Why should I prevent this from growing? What is wrong with it? We have done nothing wrong. My friend, this is an issue in which you must be ruthless.

Any love in your heart, if it is to be true and real, must resonate to the love of God that is its source. Can you openly, freely, and without the shadow of guilt invite God into a particular relationship? Your heart belongs to God, and wherever it is shared, God too is shared.

Once such an affair progresses it becomes very difficult to control. You will not be healed together, only apart. A separation that is decisive, determined, and immediate is necessary. Here is where rationalizations step in with vigor. If a physical separation is not possible, you must make known your determination to sever the relationship. Let the attraction of such an affair turn you, in your weakness, to God. Depend on his grace and strength. Christ will be sufficient for you. Such a response will benefit both parties, and if there is even the smallest bit of genuine love in the relationship, this is the only authentic attitude to adopt.

# ✦ 22
## *Some Final Advice on Friendship*

Dear friend, when you choose to cultivate a friendship, please realize the influences you are subjecting yourself to. Friendship means a sharing of mutual interests, a high regard for one another, and openness to each other's values. Be aware then of the imperfections of one another and be sure that the mutual attraction of your friendship is not based on those very imperfections.

If the attractive imperfections are strong enough to amount to sin then such a relationship should be cut off altogether. Beware of rationalizations, which assure you that you can reform such a person. It is too common to see in couples preparing to marry, one justifying the sinful habits of the other with the goal of reforming the partner after marriage. This too is rationalization. Remember, sinful friends offer sinful relationships.

## ✦ 23
## *Mortification*

Deliberate mortification, my friend, is seldom practiced today and perhaps for good reasons. In the past practices of Christians it was too often superficial, even though it sometimes involved severe austerities. At times in the early monastic fathers' and mothers' lives it even approached a kind of foolish competition somewhat like athletes vying against one another. In the more recent past, it seemed like something that was done for its own sake. Fasting, vigils, wearing hair shirts, and all sorts of penitential practices were done for strange reasons including even a kind of masochism.

Mortification and penitential exercises can have value when they are done for proper reasons and when excesses are avoided. Perhaps the more traditional practices need some modernization. The relationship of mortification to the committed life could be reviewed.

Fasting, for example, if not excessive and if one is in moderately good health, can be of value. The early Christians were urged to fast in order to save money and give alms to the poor. How easily this could be adapted today by buying less expensive foods, avoiding meat entirely or from time to time, or by practicing the laudable custom of "rice dinners." According to this custom we could have a very simple meal of rice at home instead of going out to an elaborate feast in a restaurant. The money saved is then donated to the poor. We could encourage or initiate the practice in some supermarkets of having a container into which we can drop food for the poor. People who are overweight are especially called to virtuous fasting which would be, for them, a genuine response to love of self. Aerobic exercises in moderation can also be a modern form of mortification.

What we must understand, my friend is that penitential practices have no real value when performed on a superficial ego level. They should proceed from the heart and have genuinely virtuous goals. When we call on the Lord to fill that God-shaped vacuum in which our hearts are made, then all the activities proceeding from our hearts will be Christ-oriented. Our world will be filled with Christ, in whom we will live and move and have our being. Our acts should proceed from and be motivated out of the very depths of our being—from that still point in our souls where God dwells, not from our superficial ego-centered vanities.

I remember recently seeing a family of two adults and three children on a plane when dinner was being served. The mother loudly protested the serving of meat because it was a Friday during Lent. "We are practicing Catholics," she proclaimed, "and cannot eat the meals served." She would have practiced a far more genuine mortification had she eaten what was placed before her and taken the occasion to explain to her children some principles of a truly Christian mortification. Rather, they should be grateful to God for the technology that allowed a hot meal to be served 30,000 feet in the air!

Another genuine form of Christian mortification can be found in the normal duties of our state in life. To do our job well because it is a form of service to others can be a virtuous mortification. Take the time to look at your work, whether paid or not. Does what you do fall into the categories of corporal or spiritual works of mercy? Do you serve food in a restaurant, work in a supermarket, teach children, farm, or work in a hospital? You are serving Christ as well as your brothers and sisters in these ways. Do it well for the genuine heart-felt motivation of love for God and for neighbor. This can provide you with a lifetime of genuine Christian mortification. It must be something that goes beyond a superficial level and touches and proceeds from the very heart of your being.

The ordinary healthful practices of our daily family lives can be virtuous sources of mortification: shopping expeditiously to avoid serving your family junk food; taking care to censure your own and your family's television time and programs; looking actively about you to find people who could be helped by your hospitality or friendship. Remember, my friend, that mortification helps you as well as others. What are your needs? From the answer to this question you can decide what should be your own particular form of mortification.

## ✦ 24
## *Society and Solitude*

Virtue stands in the middle, my friend, and we should seek a moderate position between overindulgence and escape from the company of others and solitude because we do not want to be bothered. Certain personalities gravitate toward the company of others. They are heart-centered or people-related, and they often seek the service professions because of that attraction. This is good. However, such people sometimes need to be reminded of the benefits of occasional solitude, even if only in a deliberate practice of meditation for twenty minutes a day.

Other types naturally enjoy being alone. Often they seek professions that allow them to spend long periods in research, working with computers, or writing. This is good too. Such people we could call brain-centered, but they need to balance their desire to be alone by reaching out to others with a deliberate involvement in society. This is especially good if it is to share the fruits of their solitude. This type of person also has to be reminded of social obligations to the community, church, neighbors, and family.

Social situations can be very valuable for us, whether we are people-centered or not. Be aware of your effect on a group, large or small. Be conscious, even when the group meets for entertainment, that you can have an influence for the good by your kindnesses, your hospitality, and by your modest sharing. Sometimes in a group situation you can be led to a kind of silent approval of sinful behavior. I watched a comedy on television on which a large audience was present to a comedian. Even in the brief time I watched it, I could see how people could be led to show approval of his impure language and topics. He even made a blasphemous reference to the Eucharist that was followed by laughter and applause. For some strange reason, every time he used an explicitly coarse word or phrase he was greeted with laughter. While it is best, of course, to avoid such entertainment altogether, if you find yourself present to it, you should not show approval simply because others do so. Bachelor or bachelorette parties supposedly associated with the reception of the sacrament of matrimony in American culture are often examples of the kind of social gathering in which committed Christians may have to take a firm and unpopular stand. The carousing associated with conventions is another powerful social situation that can drag down unwilling participants into sin. Any situation that encourages heavy drinking is to be avoided, lest one not only join in on it, but give approval by being present. Unfortunately, in the "lowest" and "highest" social levels of our culture, taking of drugs is expected to be approved or, at least tolerated. A committed Christian, my friend, will avoid these gatherings.

Regarding the benefits of solitude, much is said elsewhere. Many standard and beneficial Christian practices call for some time alone, even if it is brief, to pray, meditate, read the scriptures, or simply to take solitary walks to be with God's creation. Some of us naturally gravitate toward such practices. Others need to seek them out deliberately. All of us need them.

## ✦ 25
## *Clothing*

No culture has excelled as ours has, my friend, in providing such a variety of styles, colors, and shapes of clothing. Even many of the poor have access to this plethora, at least in our country. Most of us have clothes in our closets far beyond our capacity to use them. It is allowable to take advantage in moderation of this plenty. As in everything else, virtue stands in the middle.

Does it not seem that there should be some limits on expenditures for clothing, even among the very rich? It is alarming to see in the face of the poverty that exists in the world what prices can be paid for original dresses or tailor-made suits, to say nothing of jewelry, watches, and so on. The purpose of clothing is protection, physical modesty, and a degree of artistic enhancement, but all within reason.

Modesty in clothing varies widely in different times and cultures. Even nudity can be acceptable in certain limited circumstances for the right reasons. Modesty is possible depending on attitudes and what is commonly acceptable in a given situation. Sometimes, however, clothing is designed and used precisely to defy modesty. It is not unusual for both men and women to exhibit narcissistic behavior in their dress, to reveal as much as possible in a way that can only be interpreted as a wanton flaunting of their real or supposed physical attributes.

It is unfortunate that such people are often held up as models for society and are even prominently used in clothing advertisements. People are expected to imitate them in order to "be in style." Here, my friend, is where we should draw the line. We must not allow the superficial tastes and decisions of fashion designers to determine the bonds of good taste and Christian modestly. I do not think that anyone has ever been effectively criticized for dressing in a decorous modesty for whatever occasion. Modesty has always been beauty's best adornment. Young people must always be guided by the counsel of their elders in these matters.

## ✦ 26
## *Speaking of God*

It is really amazing, my friend, how much a doctor can learn about your health by simply looking at your tongue. Likewise, your tongue reveals a lot about your mind and your soul. It is the way we reveal to the world the inmost secrets of our being, our casual interests, our hatreds and loves, our confusions, goals, ideals, and fears. The things that we talk about the most are the things we are most concerned with.

What part does God play in your conversation? Are you comfortable speaking about God? Do you avoid God as though spirituality were a forbidden topic, something impolite or to be ashamed of? Are you afraid it might make you sound like a fanatic?

Of course there are fanatics. They speak of God in and out of season, not because they love God but because they want to push their personal beliefs into every possible situation. But if you really love God and try to experience his presence and activity in all aspects of your daily life, you will be willing to speak of God modestly, convincingly, and even boldly when it is called for.

God is the answer to most of our problems. God is the joy that permeates our celebrations. God is the consolation of our sorrows, the healing of our wounds, and the daily companion to all our activities. Cultivate a reasonable, moderate companionship with God in your daily thoughts and concerns and you will find yourself willing and able to express this in your conversation.

## ✦ 27
## Conversations

Dear friend, in the third chapter of his beautiful epistle, St. James warns us about the power of the tongue. The person who does not fall short in his conversation is perfect. How many of us could claim to be so? We dominate huge animals by simply putting a bridle in their mouths. This way we can control the whole body. We can direct the course of giant ships by merely controlling the rudder. Our tongues are like this. Small as they are, they have great powers. The tiniest match can set ablaze huge forests. The tongue is also like a fire. It can spread defilement throughout our whole body and reach out to set ablaze our environment and beyond. Men and women have tamed every kind of creature on land, in water, and in the skies but we have yet to conquer the ravaging tongue. It can be restless and filled with venom. With it we praise God, receive the body and blood of Christ, and bless our neighbors. Yet we use the same tongue for cursing, lying, and all manner of malicious commerce.

Just people speak of wisdom and their tongues utter what is right. The law of the Lord is in their hearts. Likewise the evil show the malice of their hearts through their tongues. The distinction between good and evil, my friend, is not always obvious. Sometimes we hurt people with speech in ways far more serious than physical force could do.

Parents who would be horrified at the idea of taking a stick to their children and shedding their blood often cause a deeper, more permanent harm by verbal abuse. Children are gullible and pliable and believe what they are told by adults, especially parents. A child who is constantly nagged and told she is worthless, no good, lazy, or stupid will believe it. She will grow with a low self-esteem and carry the bleeding interior wounds of such verbal abuse for years, even a lifetime.

Again, people who would never dream of inflicting physical wounds will often cause deeper hurts by ridicule or mockery. To respond to another, whether child or adult, with scornful laughter is a grievous offense against love and compassion. It prevents a person from defending himself and declares that the listener is determined not to listen to any form of explanation or self-defense. This is especially so when a group of people responds to one individual in this way. Mockery is probably the worst sin we can commit against our neighbor. Nothing is so opposed to charity. Mockery is a vice, which God detests. Most other offenses are done with at least a modicum of respect for the victim, but mockery is spewed forth with contempt and scorn.

The distinction between mockery and innocent humor is obvious. Friendly amusement at humorous predicaments that arise from natural human incapacitates are quite acceptable, even recreational. However, we must beware that it does not degenerate into mockery or hurt, especially with sensitive people. It is always wise to put ourselves in the places of people we would tease in jest. This will tell us just how far we can go.

## ✦ 28
## On Judging Others

Any judgment that we make on others, my friend, is rash. This is why Jesus so clearly warns us to stop judging, that we may not be judged. The good or evil of another's actions is attributed mainly to their intentions. We can no more know the intentions of other people than they can know ours. Have you not experienced the distressing situation of having your most innocent motives misjudged by someone else? You must then be sensitive to others, lest they receive such treatment from you.

God is the only judge, because only God can search our minds and hearts. Even then God does not really judge. When we stand before God to give an account of our lives, he will not judge us. We will judge ourselves. God neither judges nor condemns. We judge and condemn ourselves by choosing anything that is less than God. If, God forbid, we should be condemned, it will only be getting what we choose. To place our trust and hope forever in anything less than God is to choose hell. We will do this freely, if we do it. God does not judge us.

We should not judge others, even when our duty calls us to be judges. That is, in such situations, we have to let the evidence call for judgment not our own personal feelings. The law or the will of God must be the ultimate judge, and even a priest or a judge pronounces judgment only as he understands it coming from a higher source, such as evidence or a confession.

Some people habitually make rash judgments. These are bitter people whose hearts are bleeding from their own unhealed wounds. They create around themselves a world of bitterness. It blinds them and distorts their judgments. They must turn their attention inward toward their own need for wholeness, and accept their inability to justly evaluate the actions and motives of others.

Rash judgments, my friend, are usually related to our personality distortions and to the particular ways we manifest the corrupted fruits of original sin in our individual lives. Some people, often known as perfectionists, are addicted to criticizing and judging everything and everyone about them. This includes even themselves.

Anything or anyone that falls short of their standards of perfection comes under their critical judgment. They view their world (and hence create it) under these terms, often without even knowing that they are doing this. Are you such a person? Is your first reaction to someone to criticize, evaluate, or correct, even if only to yourself? Does everybody fall short of your demands for perfection? You must examine your personal responses to become aware of any such compulsive or addictive behavior. Ask yourself daily if you have judged others in your home, your job, or your personal relationships. The first step to overcome a judgmental, perfectionistic personality is to be aware of the extent to which you possess it. Then you can become, as it were, an impartial witness of your own activity and catch yourself in the process of passing judgment. You will soon be able to catch yourself even before you pass judgment. In this way, gradually your addictive attitude will begin to give way to a freedom in which you will not have to see the world as a compulsive perfectionist. When you observe that everyone (including yourself) falls short of perfection, simply accept it. You know that the world is not black or white, but most often shades of gray. You cannot change it. Accept it. Unless you are dealing with activity deliberately hurtful to others, then accept it. It is all right.

Still others, my friend, rashly judge those important to them for not being appreciative of what is done for them. These are people who serve others not because of genuine concern, but because this is the way they get personal satisfaction. If they do not receive acknowledgment for their services, they tend to become bitter, judgmental, and vindictive. Look to yourself, my friend. Do you help others because they are in need of help or because you need control over then and want them dependent on you through your services? Be aware of your motivations. Only then can you elevate them to a level of unselfish love. If you truly wish to serve others because of their needs, the service itself will be enough for you, even when it is not acknowledged.

Our own personality disorders, not really the actions of others, incline us to rash judgments. If people interfere with our efficiency or success-oriented goals, if they are not prone to appreciate our supposed specialness, or if we suspect them through our own unhealthy projections of disloyalty, we tend to make unwarranted or rash judgments. We must look to ourselves rather than to others to avoid judging. Even then we must strive to be as accepting, moderate, and forgiving as we would like others to be. If we are critical and judgmental we live in a critical, judgmental world of our own creation. If we seek to be loving, forgiving, and accepting we will live in a loving world of our own creation. This will closely resemble the world that God has created. Get real!

# ✦ 29
## *On Harming Another's Good Name*

My friend, we are guilty of the sin of detraction when we harm the good name of another by unnecessarily revealing evil abut them no matter how true it may be. There are times when evil must be revealed, but prudence must be used. Harming another's good name may very well be one of the greatest sins of modern society. It is done very often under the guise of virtue and prefaced by pseudo-excuses such as "I am no saint myself, but . . ." or "She is really a wonderful person, but. . . ."

There is an Italian saying that advises us to speak nothing but good of the dead. We must extend this also to the living. Say something good or say nothing at all. Detractions are always uttered in the absence of the person concerned, which means that he is never able to defend himself. How can we be so rash as to judge another's motivations?

I know a man who, upon hearing a detraction, would always reply, "Wouldn't it be funny if he were closer to God than we are?" There is another who invariably will insert, "He speaks well of you," into such a situation and still another who will respond, "I am sure she meant well." Such observations tend to dampen detractor's enthusiasm and are to be commended.

Someone's good name is his or her most precious asset. To destroy it mindlessly and even inaccurately is a great sin that calls for reparation. Perhaps the cruelest form of detraction is that which is offered under the guise of wit or entertainment. Public figures, of course, are subject to such treatment as an occupational hazard, but even there compassion must temper criticism.

There is also the subtle danger of unwarranted generalizations. A single act of drunkenness does not make a man a drunkard, nor does a single theft make him a thief. Always put yourself in the place of the person being victimized. It is amazing how this will temper your criticisms.

Have you noticed how often in the psalms, God is appealed to to defend the psalmist from detractors? The mockery of the arrogant and the contempt of the proud are vicious weapons that only God can counter. Do not, my friend, allow yourself to call down the wrath of God by thoughtlessly harming another's good name.

## ✦ 30
## *On Simplicity of Speech*

Let your conversations, my friend, be simple, open, and honest. Avoid pretenses and duplicity. Such things not only reflect your innermost being, they also reinforce it, for good or for evil. What causes us to take delight in scandals about others? We should rather be saddened and do what we can to help, even if only to maintain silence.

Some people delight in revealing evil done by others under the guise of frankness or honesty. While we must always speak the truth, we are not always called upon to reveal the whole truth. Examine your motives in such situations. Are you taking a perverse delight in another's faults? Does such an attitude make you feel superior? Are you unnecessarily sullying another's good name? Is this simply a way to get back at someone? To seek revenge?

Your speech reveals not another's character, but your own. So let it be frank, simple, and sincere, always coming from a sympathetic, compassionate, and loving heart.

## ✦ 31
## *On Recreation*

Your recreation, my friend, should be precisely what the word describes. It should be a re-creation, a restoration of your health in mind and body. Whether it be physical or sedentary, it should not become an obsession, because then it defeats its own purpose. In our day we are blessed with the opportunity to have more and more time for recreation. More and more of society's resources are being directed towards recreational pursuits, both outside in natural enviroments and indoors in more artificial settings. Take advantage of these things in a healthy and moderate degree for your own physical, cultural, and spiritual welfare, and for the glory of God. If you keep these two motives foremost in your thoughts and intentions, you will never go far astray in your recreational activities.

## ✦ 32

## *Questionable Recreations*

Mention should be made here, my friend, of a form of recreation always popular, but currently almost a frenzy. I am speaking of gambling, especially in the popular, gaudy casinos springing up virtually everywhere. I do not think that gambling itself is sinful, but it is often so borderline that for many people it should be avoided altogether.

Casino gambling is especially attractive to and oriented toward the retired elderly. They often have large amounts of leisure time that they cannot fill. Commercial attention is especially directed toward them to make gambling easier, more attractive, and even compulsive in subtle ways.

We have all seen people, especially the elderly, fascinated by the lure of slot machines. Sometimes they are even drawn to risk money that is needed for food or medicines. How sad it is that such zeal and energy is not directed toward God. After all, is this not what our old age should be concerned with? This kind of recreation is acceptable only on the condition that it be kept moderate. Enormous good could be done for the poor and for the needs of society if a portion of the money lost to commercial gambling establishments were put to charitable causes. If you think, my friend, that this kind of recreation is useful for you, prove to yourself that it is not harmful by limiting the time and the funds allotted to it. In addition, put aside a sum (perhaps twenty percent), not of your winnings, because that is too often not the outcome, but of what you think you can afford to gamble. This will temper your zeal and make this entertainment helpful to others.

## ✦ 33
## *Dangerous Recreations*

All things in moderation, my friend. Some forms of so-called recreation today are, by their very nature, a frenzied, irrational pursuit of empty escape. Forms of entertainment or dances often held in larger cities are of their very nature incitements toward evil. Comedians specialize in sexually explicit topics, condoning such activities and making a mockery of decent conduct. We are even able to bring such disgusting displays of intemperance and disrespect into our homes and before our children through television and videos, often under the pretense of family entertainment. It is not popular today to oppose such displays of "free speech" without being accused of censorship. Whatever you may think of this, my friend, it is always possible to avoid such programs. Do not offer your support either directly by your attention or indirectly by supporting their sponsors. Place yourself in the presence of God at your time of judgment and imagine how you will justify the time and energy devoted to such activity.

## ✦ 34
## *Lawful Amusements*

Everything leads to God, my friend. This is especially true when God is the motivation for our activity. If we keep this in mind and cherish the awareness of God's presence in all that we do, we need not fear our choice of activities. Understood correctly, this is an application of St. Augustine's saying, "Love and do what you will."

# ✦ 35
## *Daily Faithfulness*

Love, my friend, ennobles. It transforms, enhances, and elevates. The tiniest act performed in great love takes on enormous importance. On the other hand, the greatest activity done without love is not worth the ringing of a bell or the clanging of a cymbal. Great tasks strengthened by love become, of course, even greater

Don't look for greatness as the world understands that term. You probably will not be called upon to be a martyr, even though you may very well be called upon to accept great suffering in your life, both personal and with respect to those you love. What you are asked to do, my friend, is to bear with patience and love the many small trials that you experience daily. Those tiny crosses that you are given in the normal course of your life should be considered as so many opportunities to prove your love for God. An annoying cold, someone who keeps you waiting, a lost key, a cranky child, bad weather, a toothache, all these things, when embraced with love (even while trying to correct them), are pleasing to God. A simple monk one day while sweeping the kitchen floor was asked, "What would you do, brother, if it was made known to you that Jesus was coming in the next ten minutes?" "I would continue to sweep the floor," he replied. Here was a man who understood the meaning of small tasks done with love.

So, my friend, do all the great and important tasks you are called to. Feed the hungry, instruct the ignorant, counsel the doubtful, house the homeless, frequent the sacraments, and support the great endeavors your talents and resources allow. But do not forget to sweep the kitchen floor. Great opportunities to serve God are somewhat rare, small ones are frequent. Remember that our Lord charges us to be faithful in little things first. Greater things will follow. Indeed, the little things will become great. Do everything for the glory of God.

## ✦ 36
### *On Being Reasonable*

We are reasonable creatures, my friend. By this I mean that we are endowed with the capacity to be reasonable, but often we are not. The bias of our individual personalities as expressions of our distorted self love often diverts us from the path of reason. We have expectations regarding others that we would never think of imposing upon ourselves. The frequency of such activity in our daily living is alarming. Are we not being unjust and, hence, unreasonable when we call others strictly to account and yet exercise mercy and compassion towards ourselves? When we expect others to understand our criticisms and yet are sensitive and touchy ourselves? When we prefer the rich to the poor? When we give special regard to people merely because they are better dressed or more comely than others? When we cling to our own opinions and expect others to give way? We often have two standards, a strict and demanding one for others and a lenient and gentle one for ourselves. Remember, my friend, when you go against reasonableness you almost always go against love and compassion. Always try to put yourself in the other's position and then deal with them accordingly.

## ✦ 37
### *Desires*

More than you realize, my friend, your desires shape your very existence. Where your heart is, there is your treasure. When your desires are useless or vain, superficial or impossible, your existence becomes likewise. Accept what is: there God is to be found. Oh yes, you can seek to better yourself and work in that direction but do so while accepting your present situations for as long as you have it. Even to desire some good things can be a waste of time, for example, if you are sick and desire to get better so you can serve your family. Better to accept your illness, do what is necessary for healing, and meanwhile accept God's will made known in your illness and attempts to do what is required for healing. Do this lovingly and patiently. Be where you are. Blossom where you are planted. Do not be somewhere else as a product of your fancy or illusions. Do not desire some new means of serving God, but make the best use of the means you have at the moment. God will call you further only when you are where he wants you at the present moment. There are good and laudatory desires, which should not be relinquished, but they should not cause you to neglect your present status and duty. Cherish good desires and pursue them in a good and reasonable order. Meanwhile, recognize that what is is God's will for you at the present and pursue it.

## + 38
## *To Spouses*

Although there are certainly notable exceptions to this, it often seems today that the main concerns of people who desire to marry are the social arrangements, renting a hall, buying a wedding gown, and drawing lists of people to invite (as well as to exclude). These things are important, and they do serve to enhance the wedding ceremony, but are they as important as society makes them? When people ask, "Where is the wedding to be?" the answer is not the church where the vows are to be exchanged, but the function hall where the reception is to take place. Customs dictated by commercial interests are, more and more, dominating the wedding scene. Now there are showers for the bride, bachelor parties for the groom, banquets for the rehearsal night, and gifts for the attendants. These are all presented and received as absolute essentials, absorbing inordinate amounts of time and money, while the real meaning of the sacrament is obscured. Families even break up over superficial arrangements such as reserved seating, invitation lists, or reception dinners. The real meaning of the social event we call a wedding is lost in superficialities and the desire to do everything exactly as others do and as commercial interests dictate. Often the social position of the parents is determined by the elaborateness of the celebrations, and weddings are often used as ways of ascending the social ladder, even though this may mean expenditures far beyond a family's means.

Marriage is a loving bond between a couple and is compared to the union of Christ and his church. It is to be characterized by the very same love, obedience, and honor that the church has for Christ. Its sacred character is a foundation for our society and its dissolution, so common in our day, is leading to crumbling foundations and social disintegration. Its fruits are manifested in the loving support and complimentarity of the married couple, and in the ultimate expression of their love in children.

We do not today look upon women as the weaker sex, nor do we accept that the man must have the dominant role in a sacramental union. Both must love, honor, and obey the other in a holy partnership. At times this means compromise, giving way to the other's needs, and even patient personal suffering on the part of one or the other. It is a truly daring thing to place such trust in another human being, and a tribute to couples who are willing to step forward into an unknown future with such trust and love in one another. God's grace will not be lacking for them, which is the very reason marriage is a sacrament.

Children born of this holy union are themselves sacred and products of God's love as embodied in married couples. The years of care, education, and nurturing they require will be supported by the sacramental grace of matrimony. God gives a couple this promise when they seek mutual union before the ecclesial gathering of his holy people. Couples must be mindful of the graced nature of their union to take full advantage of it. They should support one another in the practice of their religion and see in one another the ultimate expression of a human and a graced friendship.

The custom of celebrating wedding anniversaries is a laudable one. It should be marked by a renewal of the sacred dedication couples make to one another.

# ✦ 39
## The Sanctity of Marital Union

The complementarity of husband and wife in marriage expresses itself fully in sexual union. When this results in the creation of a child, that expression reaches sublime heights. The child becomes the embodiment of his parents love for one another. Love, honor, and obedience to one another should be the norms governing marital sexual union. Never the product of mere lust, sexual intercourse should be an expression of mutual love, even when its intensity is not always mutually shared. Frankness, understanding, kindness, and forbearance are often called for. Modesty still has a place in marriage and depends upon the attitude, background, and desires of each individual. Here mutual respect is called for. We were made to love and everything else was made to make love possible. How concretely this truth is expressed in the context of holy matrimony.

Before monks are allowed to make the final irrevocable commitment of solemn vows they are required to have at least five years of probation and formation by living in the community and experiencing the hardships as well as the joys of monastic living. People often marry, however, after knowing each other for a relatively brief time. It is often wrongly presumed that they are formed by the ins and outs of the married life of their parents and the example of their family.

The church in the United States has introduced a very helpful program for engaged couples sometimes known as the pre-Cana program. The program is required for couples who wish to marry as Christians with church approval. Experienced people from success-ful marriages speak to them about their own trials and joys and their responses to the difficulties most common in married life. Such top-ics as financial problems, the most common cause of today's very high divorce rate, are addressed, with the opportunity to ask ques-tions and seek advice before and after marriage. Such preparation is to be highly commended. Mutual respect and honor should be the earmark of a couple's engagement. There is no such thing as a "trial marriage" as is sometimes practiced in our society. Such "unions" should be seen for what they are. There is no evidence to support such a practice as preparation for a "real marriage."

# ✦ 40
## *Advice to Widows and Widowers*

The attitude of the Church throughout the centuries has varied greatly regarding widows and widowers. The biblical advice to widows found in some of the epistles should be carefully read for the principles behind it and for whatever applications it has in the church's practice today. It must be kept in mind that St. Paul's advice to widows was meant for a special class of women who had commit-ted themselves to a way of life comparable to that of nuns in our age.

Widows and widowers today have the general approval of the Church to seek second marriages. These too are seen as sacraments every bit as much as the first marriage was. Subsequent marriages after the deaths of spouses are holy and have God's blessing. In heaven we will not be ranked according to our marital status while alive. Humility and love alone will count.

## ✦ 41
### Advice to Single People

Young men and women know well what is required of them in terms of living chastely and giving due honor to future spouses by their authentic Christian commitment. This is even more important today when forms of promiscuity are socially accepted norms. Basic to love is honor and respect, which become questionable when the full rights of marriage are casually bestowed on mere acquaintances or even engaged partners. True love does not call us to a mutual endangerment of salvation. Chastity has always been difficult for young people, and today in our amoral society it is harder than ever. The harder it is the more worthwhile is its preservation and the more abundant will be God's graces.

## PART FOUR

# *Dealing with Temptations*

## ✦ 1
### *Concerning a False Wisdom*

As people around you become aware that you are determined to live a committed Christian life, my friend, you will receive various reactions. You will not be without support from other committed Christians, especially as you seek them out in prayer groups, meditation groups, scripture discussion meetings, or other support groups. It is especially advantageous if a close friend, spouse, or other relative is active with you.

It is unavoidable, however, that you will meet with criticism. Those who criticize you will naturally be people who know nothing themselves of a committed life. Some will openly question you with smirks, raised eyebrows, or puzzled frowns and others will make fun of you subtly. Still others will be silent while bristling with disapproval. Some of these people whose lifestyles are obviously not in accord with Christian values you may simply have to disassociate yourself from.

You will be marked either as a fanatic or a hypocrite, especially when you occasionally fail through weakness or human error. They will make demands of you even Jesus does not call for. This is worldly wisdom that, together with the flesh and the devil, you can expect to challenge you.

Stand steadfast, my friend. Be like the blind man of Jericho who, when "those who were going in front" tried to silence his appeals to Jesus, simply cried out all the louder. After a while you will notice a change in your acquaintances, even a kind of respect. Do not condemn them but do not join with them either. The Lord is on your side but he loves your detractors also.

In the church today there are problems especially related to our times. However, they have been present before and even Jesus had to put up with them. I refer here to the scandals, publicly exposed, offered by the clergy and religious. Do not allow this to weaken your resolve but like the blind man "cry out all the louder." The Lord will hear you.

### ✦ 2

## *On Courage in Commitment*

Sometimes your commitment will be easy, my friend, but often in the beginning it will be hard, and you will wonder if it is worthwhile or if you can persevere. Let time be the judge. Is it better to walk with the Lord, to have Jesus as your constant companion, or to desert him for the shallow and empty company of his and, indeed, your own enemies? When you need help, ask the Lord for it. Even if you should fall through ignorance or weakness, get up again. Start over every day. Each moment is a new one and need not be held back by past failures. At first you may miss the transient and false pleasures society offers you. You may not enjoy refusing to accompany friends to questionable forms of entertainment, or refraining in joining them in the destruction of reputations, toward which gossip is often directed. Not self-righteously, but simply and honestly pursue your goal which is the Christ-life. After all, what do your critics offer you that is better? The happiest people are those who are devoted, humbly and lovingly, to the Lord. Be one of them!

## ✦ 3

# *The World, the Flesh, and the Devil*

Temptations will come, my friend. In fact, they are necessary if you are to advance at all in your commitment to Christ. They are even of use to you in determining the special virtues in which you are called to excel. If you are tempted in some particular way then it is an indication that you are especially called to the opposing virtue: If you are sorely tempted to pride, you are called to humility; If you are tempted to anger, you are called to meekness.

Spiritual masters tell us that each of us, as a result of Original Sin, has to deal in particular with one of the seven capital sins. The capital sins are not really sins in themselves but inclinations toward sin. If one is beset by the capital sin of avarice, one has a tendency to be tempted toward deeds of avarice and one is, at the same time, especially called to the virtue of generosity. It is both useful and healthy for us to realize that temptations are precisely that—temptations. They are never in themselves sins. You can be tempted, my friend, to all manner of horrible, shameful deeds but as long as they remain temptations and you do not surrender to them, they are not sinful. Rather, they are calls to virtue. Indeed the more intense they are, the greater the virtue they can prompt you to practice, but let us not be proud, since all temptations call us to humility, the foundation and the beginning of the spiritual journey.

Sometimes temptations are prolonged and severe, so much so that you wonder if you will ever be free of them. Then, in a moment, they are gone. God's grace takes over and we experience (only temporarily) a reprise. You can be sure, however, that they will return. In the beginning our temptations are usually carnal and entice us to sins of the flesh such as lust and gluttony. Then come temptations toward weariness or spiritual dryness. The more advanced we are in the committed life the more subtle are the temptations—those of pride being perhaps the most subtle. A person advanced in the committed life is not going to be enticed or deceived by obvious evil so the devil disguises himself as an angel of light. Do you remember how the devil tried to tempt Jesus? The first two temptations actually were not in themselves evil—to provide bread for himself and to experience God's care for him. It is only in the third temptation that the devil pulled out all the stops and revealed himself for what he was. "Fall down and worship me," he said, "and I will give you the whole world." We are to realize, even as Jesus did, that we already possess the whole world. (The devil is a liar, as are all temptations.) All things are already yours, the world, life, death, the present, and the future. All belong to you, and you to Christ, and Christ to God.

# ✦ 4
## *A Further Teaching on Temptations*

God chastises those whom he loves. At times this chastisement is in the form of temptation so severe that we wish he didn't love us so much. This, too, is a temptation. Recognize, my friend, your temptations as favors from God. Approach them with humility and, at the same time, with confidence in God's help. Never rest complacent. People who have overcome great temptations have been known to fall over insignificant ones due to complacency. Even if you do fall, be as merciful to yourself as God will be to you. Seek his forgiveness and begin over again. Love understands all things, and God is love.

## ✦ 5
## *Self-willed Temptations*

We must be brutally honest, my friend, in seeing the cause of some temptations. We know our weaknesses and what we must avoid. To toy with temptations by deliberately exposing ourselves to them is sinful itself. Here is where self-deception in the form of rationalization is so notable. Rationalization is the attempt to justify doing something we know to be wrong. We often use it to justify committing sins of the flesh.

## ✦ 6
## *Severe Temptations*

Pray, Jesus says, that you may not enter into temptation. Place yourself in the position of a frightened child who quickly runs into the protecting and loving arms of her mother. See God as always present to you, holding out his arms. We run to him by prayer. This is true humility, to admit our weakness and turn to God for strength. Do not look back at the temptation but only forward to your loving father. The only really effective way to deal with severe temptations is flight, flight away from the source of the evil and toward the arms of God.

## ✦ 7
## *Smaller Temptations*

Sometimes the smaller temptations are actually the harder to deal with. We are rarely tempted to murder but often have to contend with the anger that could lead to it. If a rabid dog confronts us there are usually certain definite things we can do to protect ourselves. It can be much more difficult to deal with hoards of mosquitoes on a summer night. The committed life is most often a daily battle with pesky insects rather than rabid dogs. Resist strongly severe temptations, but do not neglect the small ones.

## ◆ 8
### Further Advice Regarding Small Temptations

If you are firmly committed to following Christ, my friend, you will not be free from the myriad small temptations that assail you like insects, but you can prevent them from causing you harm. Perhaps the best way to deal with them is not through direct confrontation, but by looking over their shoulder. Let them make you look for God, who is always near. Give God your direct attention. Speak to God lovingly and simply, and experience his presence and help.

## ◆ 9
### Be Strong

The way to deal with our greatest weakness, my friend, is to practice the opposite virtue. First, give some thought to the sin itself. Are you inclined to be avaricious? Consider the generosity of God. Be grateful for all you have. Pray for those who have less. Then make a deliberate effort to do something that relates to the virtue of generosity. Give money, more than you feel is your obligation, to the needy. Give of your time more generously than you feel you have to. At first, maybe just a little more than you are inclined to. Then, if need be, increase your generosity. That way when a real temptation comes along you will be practiced in the opposite virtue.

Are you inclined to be proud? Perform small unobtrusive acts of humility. Do lowly tasks on a regular basis. You need not fill your life with them, but be familiar with them so when you are called to some significant humility, you will be able to deal with it.

Are you inclined to impatience? Go to the longest line at the supermarket. Park in the spot furthest away from the mall. Do not try yourself to the extent that you make your life miserable, but test your ability, in small ways, to practice the virtue to which you are called, especially at times when you are free from your usual temptations.

# ✦ 10
## *Anxiety*

Anxiety is probably one of the most common problems in our times. It is not only a problem in itself but is the source of many others. Discouragement, depression, and sadness all come from anxiety, and then turn back to it to increase their strength. The change of life period for both men and women leads us to reflect on the very real possibility of our own growing old, losing our faculties, or being dependent on others. Prolonged misfortune, physical illness, or chronic-insecurity resulting from low self-esteem all contribute to anxiety and its unhappy train of feelings.

How should we deal with them, my friend? This is a time to pray for the virtue of hope even, or perhaps especially, because we have so little of it. Again, the principle of seeking out the virtue opposed to our temptation comes into play. Speak to God of your complaints. Tell him as vividly as you can of your problems and feelings. Remind him of his promises to come to your aid. The very act of doing this will be a real first step out of your anxiety.

You have all that you need to face the problems that confront you. You have God. Jesus promises that he and the father will come to you and abide within you. Even without feeling this presence, act out of your faith conviction that it is true. Behave as though you are not anxious or depressed or sad. Do small or big things for yourself and for others. Even though you do not feel like it, at first in small ways then more significantly, bring yourself to act as if you were not depressed by "faking it until you make it," as the AA. program advises.

Prolonged anxiety or depression may require professional help, and even prescription medicine. However, do not depend on this too much since there is nothing you can do by yourself without God's help. Speak of this to a spiritual director or a friend as well as to God. It is all right, for a time, to depend heavily on the word and support of another. It is all right always to count on the word and support of God. He is calling you to himself in this way. Go to him.

# ✦ 11
## *On Depression or Sadness*

Sadness and depression lead to discouragement. Again, you may have to fake it till you make it, with God's help. Perform small activities at first as though you were neither sad nor discouraged. Do them as acts of faith, acknowledging that this activity is your true expression and that the depression is an aberration. Of course you will not feel like doing this, but therein lies the virtue. Continue to reach out for God's help. Do not overdo it, but refuse to lie down in the face of such weaknesses.

Spend a reasonable amount of time examining the cause of your depression. Is it possibly a physically caused problem? Get help. Is it the result of your own folly or perhaps an unresolved forgiveness issue in your recent or past life? Permit your wounds to heal and your self-esteem to grow. Always keep in touch with the source that ennobles you, that forgives you, that loves you—God.

# ✦ 12
## On Consolations

The committed life, my friend, is not all trials and sufferings. It has ups and downs, shifting movements and frequent changes. Keep your eyes on God as your anchor, your rock in times of distress, and your consolation. Let God be your light in darkness, your peace in turmoil, your relief in labor, and your joy in sadness. You may have to fake it, but know that when you act as if God has already answered your prayers and and consoled you, you are not faking it. Let nothing separate you from the love of God. Appeal to him for appreciation and gratitude.

Be aware, my friend, that feelings and emotions, as good and useful as they are, can also be deceptive, at least in terms of our interpreting them. What do they mean? What is the cause of a particular feeling, good or unpleasant? Love God and be secure in all things. Even your feelings about God and the mysteries of our faith can be misleading. When they are powerfully consoling, you can be misled into thinking that you have achieved extraordinary levels of holiness. Not infrequently such an attitude presages either a fall into sin or discouragement when the feeling does not last.

Do not seek consolations, but do not reject them. Accept them with humility and gratitude, but do not rely on them. When you are consoled, what fruits are elicited from you? Are you in a more loving attitude toward enemies? Do you make restitution for debts? Do your prayer practices benefit? You can recognize authentic consolations by their fruits. Consolations that merely bring tears to your eyes and warmth to your heart are sterile. They must also lead you to the activity of the committed life.

When I say, my friend, do not seek consolations, I mean do not seek them for their own sake. At times you will need them, and it is quite acceptable to pray for them when grieving at a beloved's death, when anxious over an illness, or when depressed or sad. In these times, pray for both perseverance and consolation, because the very act of prayer is a step toward its answer.

Consolations can, of course, increase our fervor. They can attract us to God and the things of God. They can help us realize the basic truth of our existence , that we were made for God and that our hearts will not rest until they rest in God. Consolations can provide a foretaste of this rest. Enjoy them but do not substitute them for faith, hope, and love to the degree that, when they are gone, we flounder like a boat adrift in stormy seas. Do you remember the consolations experienced by the apostles when they witnessed and even participated in Jesus' miracles, his transfiguration, and his preaching? Yet they abandoned him in his trials. How did he describe them? He said, "Oh you of little faith." Seek after faith and let consolation come as God determines.

Be aware, my friend, that there will be times when God deliberately withdraws consolations from our lives, because often we are drawn not to God but to his gifts. This is all right for beginners, but God wants to lead us to love him for his own sake and so he will withdraw the gifts to test and strengthen our love for him alone. Be grateful when this happens.

Value and appreciate consolations as gifts of God but do not put your faith in them. Put your faith in the giver, not the gifts. The book of Proverbs warns us that when we find honey, eat just enough of it. Too much may make us ill.

# ✦ 13
## Spiritual Dryness

What do we do, how should we react, my friend, when God finally does withdraw his consolations? We can almost put ourselves in the position of Jesus who, on the cross, was mocked by his enemies. "If God is on your side, come down from the cross and we will believe." You may not be able to respond in any other way than Jesus did. You may find yourself uttering his anguished cry, "My God, why have you forsaken me?" Remember, dear friend, that this cry is also a prayer.

You may feel that you have been led to a dry weary land without water. That is why there are experiences known as periods of spiritual dryness. At these times we are to recall that God is able to split the rocks in the desert and give you water as abundant as the seas. God will lead you like a sheep through the desert, and even if you walk in the valley of the shadow of death, his right hand will hold you strong. No matter how desolate, lonely, and abandoned you feel, hold onto your conviction that for God darkness itself is not dark, and night shines as the day. Speak to him then, for he is never closer than when he seems farthest away.

There are times too, dear friend, when our desolation is self-caused. Through sloth and neglect of our spiritual commitment we seem to lose contact with God. The dryness we feel is sometimes God's voice calling us back to him. Respond to him.

Be willing to accept dryness and lack of consolations for however long they last. Beat upon the heavens with your cry but, at the same time, preserve a kind of holy indifference. "God, I will endure this as long as you want me to. Just support me." St. Angela of Foligno says that this kind of prayer, the prayer which we force ourselves to make, is most acceptable to God.

The same applies to the works of mercy our committed life calls us to. The more difficult they are, the less self-love there is in their performance. Do not worry. When God wishes it, the clouds will part and you will once again find yourself basking in the warmth of his light. Only persevere!

## ✦ 14
### *An Exhortation to Persevere*

St. Bernard reminds us that beginners in the committed life easily loose courage when those very consolations which drew them to God in the first place are withdrawn. Our spiritual masters tell us that we need, in our weaknesses, some kind of spiritual consolation. This experience leads us to reject worldly pleasures and teaches us to rejoice in heavenly values. But when the heavenly consolations are also taken away, we are suspended in a kind of limbo that is neither heaven nor earth. In these times we realize our true selves. We are left only to our own resources. What do we do? How do we feel and act?

Bernard's companion, Geoffrey, once found himself in a state of dryness. When a friend took him aside to ask what ailed him, Geoffrey replied that he felt he would never know joy again. The friend confided in their spiritual father, St. Bernard, who immediately went to a nearby church to pray for Geoffrey. Geoffrey meanwhile, overcome with sadness, fell into a troubled sleep. After a while St. Bernard rose from his knees and Geoffrey rose from his sleep. His friend was amazed to see his smiling face and serene attitude. When he asked what had happened, Geoffrey told him, "I thought that I should never see joy again, now I think I shall never be sad again."

Note, my friend, what God does. He gives us joy and consolation as a foretaste of heaven to wean us from earthly attachments. Then he withdraws the consolations so that we may seek more solid food than the spiritual candy hitherto given us. At this time we may also be visited by physical illness, family problems, social distress, and all sorts of unpleasant temptations, even ones we thought we had definitely conquered. We must not lose confidence. The night is darkest when we are closest to dawn. Pray for perseverance. Talk with a spiritual friend. Enlist his prayers and deliberately ask him to console and encourage you.

God is allowing you these trials to encourage you to strive for the committed life and the eventual joys of heaven. The world, the flesh, and the devil allow you the same trials to drag you down. This is a time when you can make great progress in your spiritual pursuits.

When you are afflicted with spiritual dryness it is wise, within limits, to be good to yourself. Along with your earnest prayers and the support of your spiritual director or friend, allow yourself some legitimate rest and relaxation. Be moderate in your labors and refresh your soul, mind, and body as well as you can.

St. Francis was oppressed by sadness and spiritual dryness for two years. He could not find any comfort, even in prayer. He felt abandoned by God. Suddenly, in one moment, God restored his former joys on an even deeper level. When you have such an experience, dear friend, you will realize that even though you were then unaware of it, you were never closer to God. Expect these trials. Do not fear them, but allow them to humble you and force you to depend on your faith in God alone.

◆  ◆  ◆

## PART FIVE

*How to Renew and Preserve
Your Commitment to Christ*

## ✦ 1
## *The Need for Renewal*

I would like to share with you, dear friend, some exercises that are directed toward a renewal and strengthening of your commitment to Christ. In addition to your daily devotions, frequent reception of the sacraments, and the active loving responses you are called to exercise in your Christian commitment, it is helpful, even necessary, to give yourself a special time specifically directed to renew and strengthen that commitment.

Depending on your circumstances, take the time to make a retreat—a few days, a weekend, a day of recollection, or even only a couple of afternoons at home. Allow yourself a greater solitude than usual and a space set apart from your usual preoccupations.

## ✦ 2
## *The Value of Your Commitment*

You may follow these suggestions as a reflective meditation, or you may use them as topics for a heart to heart, personal conversation with the Lord.

Consider or speak to Jesus about the meaning of your commitment to him as his follower. What does this mean in the concrete living out of your daily life? Tell him that you resolve never to deny this commitment by word or action. Should you fall to any degree because of human frailty, promise him that you will reach out for his grace to begin again. You will do this as often as necessary. Reflect for a few minutes or speak to Jesus about the value of such a commitment. How wonderful it is to be called to such a life and to respond to that call. Tell the Lord honestly, openly, and humbly how sacredly you value your commitment to him. Allow yourself to feel the awe of this privilege. Speak to the Lord of your desire to be aware of his calling, of how much you value his interest in you and his love for you. Ask him to make you more sensitive to the pull of that love.

Ask the Lord to help you to understand what a difference his call makes in your life. Where would you be spiritually without that grace? What would your life be like? How often have you been aware of significant differences in your life and lifestyle because of your commitment to respond to his graces? Offer God a brief prayer thanking him for his goodness to you and asking him for the graces to persevere in your response to that goodness.

## ✦ 3
## *An Examination of Conscience*

Spend a reasonable amount of time reflecting on or talking to God about the three loves in your life—love for God, love for self, and love for others. You may want to do this all at once or in three seperate sessions. This need not be done on your knees or in a church: you can do it while going for a walk, driving your car, waiting for a bus, or before you go to sleep. Decide specifically just when you will do this and faithfully carry it out within one or two days' time.

Place yourself in the presence of God. He is there wherever you are. Acknowledge him. Ask him to help you understand the ways you have grown spiritually, as well as your shortcomings. Seek to do this for God's glory and the coming of his kingdom. Now prepare yourself to consider calmly and peacefully how you have acted toward God, yourself and your neighbor.

## ✦ 4
## *Toward God*

The foundation of your committed life is to live in such a way that you never sever your relationship with God. The highest form of relationship with God is a form of love known as "union of wills." You will only what God wills. Thus you will have a special regard and even love for every manifestation of God's will. Do you feel this way regarding the Ten Commandments? Do you see them as restrictions on your activity or as directives freeing you from the bondage of self-love and the slavery of material attachments? Are you complacent in small things that you know lessen the strength of your commitment to God? What is your attitude toward prayer?

## ✦ 5
## *Your Neighbors*

To be totally given in love to God, my friend, you must first mentally accept that spiritual exercises strengthen your understanding of God's love, and convince you that God's love is your highest good. Then, by the strength of your conviction, you allow this belief to enter your heart until you feel it. Then you prompt this feeling to bring forth the work of your hands in the service of your neighbor.

Do you recognize that your neighbor includes those closest to you? Spouse, children, parents, family? Do you recognize that neighbor includes even your supposed enemies? Do you accept the fact that neighbor includes even those faceless multitudes you know of only through the disasters reported daily through the mass media? What are you doing about it? Do you deliberately seek to feel compassion for the suffering of your immediate world? Of the whole world? What do you experience in others that seems to you the most difficult or disagreeable? How do you respond? Are you too ready to think or speak ill of your neighbor? Do you ever find yourself rejoicing in the misfortunes of others?

## ✦ 6
## *Yourself*

Self-love, my friend, is a virtue. In it we embrace a oneness in ourselves. We do not allow contradictions by doing things which are self-destructive. We seek for ourselves the fullness of our being and the glory of our destiny, which is eventual perfect union with God.

Are you too strict with yourself? Too lenient? Do you engage in self-destructive behavior such as smoking, overeating, or insufficient exercise? Are you careless about your health? Do you neglect seeking professional medical advice when situations call for it?

You cannot really love others unless you love yourself. We are commanded to love our neighbor as we love ourselves. To love yourself is to orient yourself toward God in every aspect of your body and soul. God's will for you, in every situation, is that you grow in love, wisdom, and grace. This is not something that just happens to you. You must actively pursue it. How do you do this on a daily basis? Most of the negative problems that affect you—low self-esteem, job burn out, poor health—usually result from neglect of true self-love. Do you seek to enjoy the legitimate pleasures God gives you? Do you take advantage of the opportunities you have to grow in the spiritual life and in the active apostolate?

## ✦ 7
### *A Look at Your General Attitude*

Here, my friend, is a brief and simplified way to review the advice given above. Ask yourself and talk to God about how you have acted in terms of loving God, yourself, and others. Speak about your fear of and hatred for anything that could lessen your Christ-commitment. Are you overly concerned with material possessions and pleasures? What do you really hope for? Are your primary goals earthly things? What causes you sadness? Does it have to do with transitory worldly things? Where do you find real joy? Does the praise of God's glory find a real and significant place in your plans and desires?

## ✦ 8
### *More on General Disposition*

Having taken this deliberate scrutiny of your spiritual life and the condition of your soul, my friend, now draw some conclusions about yourself before God. If you see some progress, frankly admit it, and thank God. If you feel that your progress has been less than it should be, admit your neglect in responding to God's graces. Ask God's pardon. Offer him all that you are, warts and all, and beg for fidelity, constancy, and perseverance.

## ✦ 9
## *Considerations*

Here are five specific considerations for you to talk to God about or to meditate upon. Consider each one for at least ten minutes, longer if convenient. In each case, place yourself in the presence of God. Ask God's help.

## ✦ 10
## *The First Consideration: Your Own Nobility*

Your heart was made for God. You are created in God's image and likeness. You are a child of God, redeemed by the blood of Jesus Christ and sanctified, not by your own efforts, but by the action of the Holy Spirit. You have a mind which can reach up toward God and a will which can embrace him. Why, when you come from such a magnificent background, do you allow yourself to be concerned with anything less than God? You know you are called to eternal life with God. How can you be really affected by anything else? Know and appreciate your origin, your call and your destiny.

## ✦ 11
## *The Second Consideration:*
## *The Beauty of a Good Life*

If, my friend, you are ever to have any semblance of happiness in this world, it will only be through your active pursuit of the next.

There is no middle way. You either seek after God and pursue him, or you sell your soul to the devil. A saint once said that the way to heaven is heaven. You create your own world by living in Godly virtues or earthly passions. A loving person lives in a loving world of his own creation. An angry person creates around herself an angry world. How beautiful it is to seek to be loving, patient, humble, forgiving, generous and compassionate. You know from experience how these virtues enhance your life even here on earth. You know too how the opposite vices destroy you and make you, and all around you, miserable.

## ✦ 12
## *The Third Consideration: Good Example*

What a wonderful thing it is that the Church preserves for us the memory of the saints. From the very beginnings of the Church until even today, there is a vast array of people who have so incorporated the Christ-life into their own lives, that each of us can find, not only one or two, but many to relate to, both by example and through their intercession. The ways the saints have responded to God's calling are beautiful, dramatic, sad, beguiling, clever, commonplace, simple, humorous, frightening, compelling, heroic, and inventive. There is something in them for each of us.

Look also to the saints of today. We are living in another age of martyrs in Latin America, Indonesia, Algeria. We might even know some of the heroic individuals who have laid down their lives in these places in the service of God, and still others who labor daily to further God's kingdom at great personal cost.

Look about you and see examples of perseverance under great trial by people you know: the sick, the elderly, the poor, and those dedicated to them. Ask these people for their prayers. Imitate their virtues. Be grateful to God for them. Our call and the graces we are given to pursue it are not different from theirs.

## ✦ 13
### *Fourth Consideration: God's Love for Us*

Our God is a personal God. He is not only the God of Abraham, the God of Jacob and the God of Isaac, he is the God of William, of Abdul, of Sylvia, of Paul, of Denis, of Kurt, of Manuel, and of Mimi! His intense desire to personalize his love for each of us is what prompted the Eternal Word to come down from his heavenly throne and take upon himself our human nature. God is personally only as far away from you as you are from yourself. His availability is intense, immediate, loving, and constant. He dwells within you!

## ✦ 14
### *Consider God's Eternal Love for You*

You exist, my friend, because God loved you before you existed! From all eternity you have been in the mind of God, in the love of the Divine Word, and in the plans of the Holy Spirit. God says to you what he says to all his chosen: "I have loved you with an everlasting love." Appreciate this.

## ✦ 15
## *General Conclusions: A Prayer*

Dear Lord, you have brought me to this place in my committed life. You have made me like a tree planted by flowing waters that yields its fruit in due season and whose leaves never fade. Thank you. My devotions, my resolutions, my efforts to love are all your ways of giving me yourself. Whatever happens to me in this life, I will remain steadfast in my pursuit. What a truly blessed thing it is to know that I have your grace and put my trust in you.

I acknowledge, dear Lord, my weaknesses, but I know that when I am weak then I am strong because I must put my trust in you. Give me, Lord, your wisdom to see my world, my life, and my resolves as pleasing to and inspired by you. Help me to know that I am never alone, and grace me to be an aid to others by my example, my prayers, and my loving services.

If it helps you, dear friend, write this or a similar prayer out. Add to it whatever you wish. You may even specify particular resolutions you are making as a result of your meditations at this time to strengthen and renew your Christ-commitment.

## ✦ 16
## *Remember*

Remember, my friend, the graces God gives you on a daily basis. Actively reach out to receive them. You can do this peacefully and joyfully simply by offering a brief prayer of a few words often during the day. In the middle of your conversations, your work, your recreation, peacefully say something like, "Lord I offer myself to you" or "Lord, be with me." Then gently and without straining either mind or body, go about your day.

# ✦ 17
## *Dealing with Discouragements*

You will not be without discouragements, dear friend. Some of them will even come from people who are close to you, who should be supporting your resolves to remain close to God. They will say, "Forget your devotions. Are you some kind of religious fanatic? You people are all hypocrites! Let it go just for today." Of course you will be moderate in the time and effort you give to specific devotions. Do not feel that you always have to "get them all in." Do not, from some sense of guilt, feel that you must take on every devotion that comes your way. The church offers many kinds of prayer, meditation, and religious practice. We should not feel obligated to partake in them all, because they are offered to all people, each with different expressions of their commitment. Take what appeals to you. Change them when you no longer feel they are effective.

# ✦ 18
## *Conclusion*

Be honest and frank to others, my friend, about your commitment to Christ and your resolves to live that commitment. Never be pushy or obnoxious. If you see that someone is annoyed by your dedication, persevere in your private practices and pray for him. Do not judge. Confess openly and simply your conviction that any life not lived for God's sake and to do his will is empty and vain. Yet do not be preachy. Rather let your example and a few honest statements serve to express your faith. Only continue to persevere in your committed life. May the Lord Jesus be ever present in your goings and comings, and to him with the Father in the graciousness of the Holy Spirit be all honor and glory. Amen.

# Also by William A. Meninger

*The Loving Search for God*
*Contemplative Prayer and The Cloud of Unknowing*

"Would that this little book had been in my library 30 years ago, as I struggled to appreciate that 14th-century anonymous masterpiece, *The Cloud of Unknowing*. Now that I have Fr. Meninger's warm and winning guide, I can reread *The Cloud* with appreciation instead of resistance. . . . Fr. Meninger's discussion of Psalm 22 is alone worth the price of the book. He invites us to awaken to the healing fact that the loving search is, first of all, Gods search for us. Just read it, and you'll feel the power of love stealing over you."

—*The Living Church*

"Using the 14th-century spiritual classic *The Cloud of Unknowing* as both a jumping-off place and a sustained point of reference, Meninger, a Trappist monk and retreat master, does a powerful, even stunning job of explaining contemplative prayer and making it approachable for any seeker. In a nurturing, practical, and easy-to-understand manner, and with an obvious affection for his subject, Meninger deals with the yearning search for God through prayer and with the distractions that can impede it—unforgivingness, will, distortions of imagination, memory, and intellect. The result, filled with humor and built by means of good, solid language that flows beautifully, is an excellent guide for anyone interested in deepening his or her Christian prayer life."

—*Publishers Weekly*

*The Process of Forgiveness*

"Will appeal to readers seeking a popular introduction to techniques for dealing with hurt."

—*Booklist*

"Going beyond Lewis Smedes's classic *Forgive and Forget,* Meninger makes abundant use of scripture, to help readers understand forgiveness, and he recommends prayer to help them experience it."

—*Publishers Weekly*
Religion Bookline

"Father Meninger unites in this very readable work the ideas of Elizabeth Kübler-Ross on death and dying, the enneagram personality characteristics and contemplative prayer through the centering prayer technique. Acknowledging that forgiveness is probably the most difficult demand Jesus makes of His followers, he presents and orderly process to enable us to do so. This is a serious effort by an experienced spiritual director written in a very readable fashion, full of stories and personal experience. Hard to forgive? This book will help you."

—*Columbian Mission*

*Bringing the Imitation of Christ*
*into the Twenty-First Century*

"This book succeeds admirably in what it sets out to do: to intro-
duce Christians, in a way that engages them personally, to the rich
resources which the *Imitation of Christ* offers those who seek a practical path for approaching God. Those unacquainted with the original will find this book most helpful; others will find here a useful,
readable resource for enriching their personal lives and ministry."

—*Catholic Library World*

"William Meninger freely acknowledges that some features of
Thomas à Kempis' *Imitation of Christ* no longer win acceptance in
the modern church but argues that other elements of the work are
timeless. In particular he tries to express, in modern idiom, the
*Imitation*'s emphasis on the need to consider the motivation behind
our action and the necessary singleness of mind in our Christian pil-
grimage. Sometimes there is need for adaptation and reemphasis,
sometimes for outright omission and rewriting. . . . By such means
the gulf the *Imitation* set between the world and the religious life is
bridged; the lack of any significant emphasis on issues of social jus-
tice is redressed and modern understandings of the self-identity of
both religious and lay people of our own day are better reflected."

—Feed the Minds
*Theological Book Review*